THE BRAVE

CONQUERING THE FEARS THAT HOLD YOU BACK

HAYLEY & MICHAEL DiMARCO

Revell
a division of Baker Publishing Group
Grand Rapids, Michigan

Hungry Planet

Published by Revell
a division of Baker Publishing Group
P.O. Box 6287, Grand Rapids, MI 49516-6287
www.revellbooks.com

Printed in the United States of America

Library of Congress Cataloging-in-Publication Data
DiMarco, Hayley.
      The brave : conquering the fears that hold you back / Hayley and
      Michael DiMarco.
            p.   cm.
      "Hungry Planet."
      ISBN 978-0-8007-3305-6 (pbk.)
      1. Fear—Religious aspects—Christianity. 2. Anxiety—religious
aspects—Christianity. 3. Courage—Religious aspects—Christianity.
4. Peace of mind—Religious aspects—Christianity. I. DiMarco,
Michael. II. Title.
BV4908.5.D56 2012
241'.4—dc23   2012006216

Unless otherwise indicated, Scripture quotations are from GOD'S WORD®. © 1995 God's Word to the Nations. Used by permission of Baker Publishing Group.

Scripture quotations labeled ESV are from The Holy Bible, English Standard Version® (ESV®), copyright © 2001 by Crossway, a publishing ministry of Good News Publishers. Used by permission. All rights reserved. ESV Text Edition: 2007

Scripture quotations labeled NIV are from the Holy Bible, New International Version®. NIV®. Copyright © 1973, 1978, 1984, 2011 by Biblica, Inc.™ Used by permission of Zondervan. All rights reserved worldwide. www.zondervan.com

Scripture quotations labeled NLT are from the Holy Bible, New Living Translation, copyright © 1996, 2004, 2007 by Tyndale House Foundation. Used by permission of Tyndale House Publishers, Inc., Carol Stream, Illinois 60188. All rights reserved.

The internet addresses, email addresses, and phone numbers in this book are accurate at the time of publication. They are provided as a resource. Baker Publishing Group does not endorse them or vouch for their content or permanence.

Published in association with Yates & Yates, LLP, Literary Agents, Orange, California.

12   13   14   15   16   17   18   7   6   5   4   3   2   1

CONTENTS

THE BRAVE

Hi, I'm Hayley, and the world scares me. I'm sure that if a natural disaster happens anywhere near me, I'll die. I hate earthquakes, tornadoes, and hurricanes, and I will never live where those things happen. I just know robbers are going to break into my house if the doors aren't locked or mug me if I walk on the streets at night. I'm afraid of mean girls—well, any girls, really. I know I will be the one in however many who dies in a plane crash. I'm crazy scared of big, bad things in this world, and I've been that way all my life. My mom taught me to keep the car full of gas and my passport up-to-date in case we ever have to flee the country in a hurry. So I'm ready.

Pain hurts, and I do all I can to avoid it. Comfort is my best friend—oh, how I love it! I will do whatever it takes to get it. So "brave" would not be a word ever used to describe me.

HAYLEY DiMARCO

Hi, I'm Michael, and I'm an addict. Life overwhelms me, and I am afraid of being out of control, and so I gamble on cards, dice, and in a way, relationships. I do whatever I'm best at, in order to hide from reality. I have a fear of failure. Failure is the end of my control and success; I have to be accepted by people or I'm a failure. And failure is not an option, so I'll do whatever I can to please people or just get away from them. My life didn't turn out how I wanted it to, I'm miserable and have no will to stand up for what I believe, and so I turn to addictive actions. I self-sabotage and destroy the life I have so that I can stop the pain that I fear so much. I fear discomfort so much that I'll eat an entire extra large pizza in one sitting just to stop the pain. In fact, if I'm not feeling good, I pretty much can't do anything but eat, watch sports, and play video games. There are times when the world leaves me feeling hopeless and unable to do anything about it, so I retreat into solitude and isolation.

What you've just read were our true feelings when we were unable to be brave in our lives. For both of us, life was out of control, and "brave" would not have been a description of us. We were letting the world win, seeing no hope and finding no strength for the job of life. It wasn't until we learned some things about this life and the next that we finally were able to see things as they really are and to gain the bravery we needed to not only deal with our crazy fears but to continually conquer them.

The natural tendency of all of us humans is to fear. It's about self-preservation. Self-preservation is the most important thing in life, because without it, well, there is no life. So when things get rough, dangerous, or uncertain, humans fear the worst.

Can you relate? Do you ever doubt the best and fear the worst? Are you stressed? Do you worry? When you want to just give up, stop the fight, and hide in your room, you have lost your bravery. When pain and suffering are knocking on your door and threatening to whup you upside the head and you are going crazy with just the thought of it all, you need to be brave.

Everyone has times in their lives when God just doesn't come through the way we expected, when heaven even sounds empty, if not angry. That's really what's at the root of all your fear, doubt, worry, and stress: this sense that your world is a mess and no one cares—or at the very least, no one who can do anything about it.

Fear tells you that God has checked out, that his anger is stronger than his love, and that you are doing this thing called life all alone. Fear isn't just about the inability to charge into battle, but it's about your inability to cope with everyday life and your desire to just give up. And that's where being brave comes in.

The Brave aren't genetically different from the rest of us; they just have learned to see things differently. They know the answer to the question "Why?" and because of that they have the courage to face their fears and their doubts. The Brave have faith—not in themselves but in their God. When everything around them says he's checked out and not to be trusted, their faith kicks in and takes over. That's because they fear God more than they fear anything else in this world. That doesn't mean they are scared of him, but they know his power, his ability, and his love, and they know that they're bigger than even the biggest pain or trouble they could ever face.

With just a simple acceptance of what God wants to give you, you too can have the bravery you've been missing. When you learn the truth about your life from the perspective of the divine, things change in a major way. For us they sure did.

I am still Hayley, but most days the world doesn't scare me anymore. In fact, if a natural disaster happens anywhere near me, I know that whatever will happen will be the best thing for my life. I still hate earthquakes, tornadoes, and hurricanes, but they don't scare me or control me. I know their power, but I know even more the power of the one who controls them, and I trust him. I know there are bad people in this world, but I know that God is our protector (see Ps. 5:11) and he can be trusted to be my protection. I had been afraid all of my life, but now fear has lost its power. I fly all the time, and I am not afraid of crashing or dying, because I know that God's will, whatever it is, will be the best thing for me.

HAYLEY DiMARCO

I'm Michael, and I'm an addict by nature but a resister by faith. Life tries to overwhelm me, but since I now know it's not my show to run, I can be brave in the face of it all. I am not afraid to fail anymore. Failure actually just means I'm one step closer to the goal. Most days now, I am more concerned with pleasing God than pleasing people, so if you don't like me, that's okay. My life didn't turn out how I imagined it would, but I'm happy, very happy. I don't like discomfort and would like to get out of it as quickly as possible, but I do it not by eating but by turning it all over to the God who can handle it better than I can. I still get recharged by being alone, but I also love being with the ones I love and get energy from that as well.

That's the way things are for us today, at least most days. We still have our cowardly moments, but we've come a long way in the past few years. We've seen some amazing acts of God and learned some incredible things about him. He can be trusted, we know that for sure. And when you know that for sure, *brave* will be a description of you. Your fear and doubt is about your inability to manage your world. We can totally relate to that. Life gets out of control a lot. Lots of dangerous things, stupid things, and downright ugly things can happen to you. But the one thing we are sure of is the one thing that never changes, and that is God's goodness and power.

In *The Brave* we want to convince you of that and reveal to you God's hand in your life. We want you to know that you aren't alone and that what you can't control, he can. In the chapters that follow, you are going to get the truth about who God is and why hard things happen in your life. We are going to talk about your pain and your suffering and about his. We are going to talk about what you fear that makes sense and what you fear that is pointless. What we hope to do is to give you all the bravery you need to deal with all the stuff in your life with calm, peace, and hope.

THE BRAVE QUIZ

Take a look at this list and be honest with yourself about how much you believe each one. If you agree with the statement at least 51 percent of the time, mark it with a T for True. If not, then leave it blank.

___ 1. I'm a worrier.

___ 2. I'm self-confident.

___ 3. I'm shy.

___ 4. I have to be in control.

___ 5. I'm insecure.

___ 6. I have no fear.

___ 7. I doubt I'll ever be successful.

___ 8. I don't need anyone.

___ 9. I'm afraid of failing.

___ 10. I love taking risks.

___ 11. I'm scared of natural disasters.

___ 12. I have amazing self-control.

___ 13. I won't do a thing if it scares me.

___ 14. I love keeping the rules.

___ 15. I wish I were more brave.

___ 16. I've been called arrogant.

___ 17. I worry about losing my loved ones.

___ 18. I hate rejection.

Give yourself one point for each **ODD** number you marked as True: _____

Give yourself one point for each **EVEN** number you marked as True: _____

NOW LET'S SEE WHAT ALL THIS MEANS.

2–9 ODD NUMBERS TRUE: SCARED—We are defining being scared as letting being afraid control you. Being scared is being full of fear. It is seeing the things that are fearful as important in your life and even as defining your life. "I'm afraid of flying, so I won't get on an airplane" is a statement a scared person makes. Hayley knows all about this. Most of her life she was scared of flying. She was sure that any plane she got on would crash and she would die a torturous and horrible death. She would do anything she could not to have to fly. Each time she did have to fly, she would panic and freak out the entire flight. So she knows about being consumed with fear, and it's no fun. The lack of brave in a life is horrific. It gives fear the main stage in life. But that doesn't have to be the final story; it wasn't for Hayley, and it doesn't have to be for you. You can take charge by giving God control and changing the way you live. Turn scared into brave!

2–9 EVEN NUMBERS TRUE: SELF-CONFIDENT—Self-confidence is an amazing thing. It makes life more manageable. It gives you self-control, certainty, and the ability to be brave. Self-confident people look at scared people and think, "That makes no sense." Their confidence comes naturally; they are sure of their abilities, their skills, and their strengths. They can take care of situations and handle whatever comes. Their lives exhibit much bravery and success, but it isn't a constant. They can have moments of fear, doubt, and insecurity. Of course, their strong sense of self can override most of that and get them back on top. The trouble with self-confidence, however, is in the word *self*. Confidence in that which is human is weak at best, because humans are broken, sinful, and imperfect. We all are. And while self-confidence has its amazing traits, it can also quickly plummet in the face of failure or rejection, or just as bad, it can become deceptive, self-important, a cover-up for insecurities, or just plain prideful. Self-confidence sounds better than it really is.

1–2 TOTAL TRUE: THE BRAVE—People who are a part of the Brave are neither scared nor self-confident but put their confidence in God. They know they can do anything if God is willing. They trust that no matter what might come, God is in control. They trust his goodness so much that even if the mountains should fall into the sea, they will not fear (see Ps. 46:1–2). That's because they put their confidence in the perfection of God rather than in the imperfection of humans. There's something supernatural about the Brave. That's because being brave is next to impossible without God. And that's the secret to all the brave that you need: brave doesn't come from within; it comes from a faith in the one who can save you, who has only the best planned for you and the grace to give it to you.

The Brave aren't perfect people with perfect skin, perfect smiles, and perfect muscles. They aren't an elite Delta Squad trained to withstand extreme conditions and insurmountable odds. The Brave are not extraordinarily gifted people who fearlessly go where no man has gone before.

The Brave are imperfect, broken people who, through no strength of their own, endure all things, suffer well, replace worry with faith, and swap doubt with trust. The Brave are simply those who have learned their own limitations and are okay with them, leaving all that they lack to the one who lacks nothing. The Brave are the faithful whose lives don't revolve around themselves but revolve around their God, who is worthy of all their attention and praise.

The Brave have no respect for the feelings that threaten their belief but all the faith imaginable in the power and the love of their God. Feelings like worry, doubt, fear, dejection, self-condemnation, self-hatred, envy, and bitterness—none of these make sense to the brave mind because these call God a liar, calling into question his faithfulness, kindness, forgiveness, justice, and love. The Brave are those who have discovered the contradictions in their feelings, thoughts, and beliefs and have worked hard to let go of fear and let God be who the Bible says he is. They have given all things to God, allowing the Holy Spirit to infiltrate and inform all of their thoughts and choices, actions and inactions because of their complete trust in God.

All this means that the Brave know who God is and what God can do, as well as who they are and what they can't do. So the Brave are not controlled by the waves of their emotions or the danger of their circumstances. Notice we said *controlled by*. The Brave still have emotions, feelings, and even fears, but they quickly surrender them to God instead of giving in to them. That means they don't freak out when everyone else freaks out. They don't panic when all looks lost. They don't fall into a depression when life isn't all they thought it would be. They don't dwell on the negative, doubting the kindness and sovereignty of God, but they believe, they hope, and they count on his mercy, power, and grace to get them through even the toughest storm. They don't see life the same way the doubter does. They aren't worried about what mean people think, what evil people do, or what angry people say. They trust the words of the prophet Isaiah when he said, "'Don't say that everything these people call a conspiracy is a conspiracy. Don't fear what they fear. Don't let it terrify you.' Remember that the LORD of Armies is holy. He is the one you should fear and the one you should be terrified of. He will be a place of safety for you" (Isa. 8:12–14). That is why they are considered the Brave—not because of their own strength but because of his.

Since it has nothing to do with who you are, you too can be part of the Brave. The only strength you need to have is the strength to believe in a God who can be all that we need him to be. But maybe you say, "I already believe, but that hasn't helped me with the fear in my life. That hasn't made rejection any easier or failure any funner (yes, my grammar fails sometimes). How can I believe enough to become a part of the Brave?" What a good question. So glad you asked. The good news is that if you already believe, then all it will take to get brave into your life is a minor tweak or two, an adjustment in your belief, a reminder of the truth that you know in your heart of hearts. The brave you're looking for isn't that far away; in fact, it can be yours in a matter of moments. Bravery may have escaped you all these years just because you didn't know one little thing about who God is that will change your entire perspective on who you are. That's what happened to us. We suddenly saw God as sovereign—powerful enough to be in control of everything. We saw his hand in everything in our lives, and we trusted that hand. All we had to do was to understand this one thing about God, and an entire avalanche of truth started pouring down on us and giving us more bravery than we had ever imagined. And it came without an inflated view of ourselves or some amazing kung fu skills.

We aren't writing to you from the perspective of people who have always had it all together but totally the opposite—we have been complete messes, consumed with worry, fear, doubt, addiction, idolatry, anger, and the list goes on. But we have found the secret to

contentment that Paul talks about in Philippians 4:11. The life God has given us, the pain, the suffering, the isolation, the failure, the bad stuff as well as the good— all of it is fine with us, because we know who has everything under control. We are the Brave because we believe in a perfect God with a perfect plan, and we believe he has a perfect plan for you too. So if you are ready to become a part of the brave followers of the only true God, let's get this thing going!

If you aren't ready for that kind of ride, we understand how you feel, and we have something just for you. You get to flip ahead to the end of the book. The next chapter has a little something to help you better understand the God we are talking about and counting on for all the bravery that this life will ever require. Know God and know brave. Know fear? Then let us introduce you to the God who loves, and see if what you learn about him doesn't just change your entire life today.

CHAPTER

1

*T*HE BRAVE ARE FEW, AREN'T THEY? Not many people can be counted on to do what is right, to fight for the rights of the weak, to stand up in the face of the bully, to refuse to cower when called on to make a difference, even if only a small one. The Brave make headlines. The Brave change cultures. The Brave are to be envied. But the Brave aren't just the ones who fight against the odds or who run into burning buildings to save puppies. The Brave aren't just tough guys who fight against the dictators of the world and the dictators of their emotions as well. The Brave are people like you who endure the anger of friends with love and compassion, who live in a less than perfect family but don't return drama with drama, who don't give up when others say "there's no hope." They are people who have enough faith to pray for help when no help can be seen. They resist temptation when they desperately want to give in.

Bravery takes place not just on the outside where all can see it but on the inside as well, in your thoughts and your beliefs.

THE BRAVE HAVE FAITH—faith that what they believe in makes all the pain and fear in the world endurable, and faith that what they have to do is doable because of this belief. **THE BRAVE AREN'T EASILY KNOCKED AROUND.** They don't cower in fear; they aren't consumed with worry, doubt, or anxiety, because those are the opposite of faith. **THEY HAVE A CONFIDENCE** about them that makes them easy to be around.

THE BRAVE ALSO HAVE CONVICTIONS. When Francis Scott Key wrote the poem that would become "The Star-Spangled Banner," he wrote about "the land of the free and the home of the brave." "The brave" were the men and women of our new country who believed so strongly in their freedom that they were willing to endure long, hard winters with little comfort or ease and long, hard battles that would threaten to take the lives of everyone who fought in them. These colonists believed so much in their new country that they had the bravery to fight against the odds. Bravery, in order to endure, has to come with some kind of belief—belief in what it is that the Brave stand for, fight for, or endure. *The Brave must believe.*

So the question is, what do you believe in? Is your belief strong enough to make you one of the Brave? The truth is that most of us lack courage from time to time. We worry, we fear, we get stressed out—all because we don't have enough faith.

BRAVERY IS FUELED BY BELIEF, but belief in what? You can have belief in yourself and your abilities. This kind of self-esteem, or self-confidence, can go a long way. A lot of battles have been won by confident people who believed something so strongly that they were willing to die for it. In the movie *Braveheart*, William Wallace calls on this kind of bravery when he says,

> I am William Wallace, and I see a whole army of my countrymen here in defiance of tyranny. . . . Aye, fight and you may die. Run and you'll live. At least a while. And dying in your beds many years from now, would you be willing to trade all the days from this day to that for one chance, just one chance to come back here and tell our enemies that they may take our lives . . . but they'll never take . . . our *freedom*![1]

The desire to fight for what you believe in is such a powerful one that it leads people all over the world to amazing feats of bravery. But it can also lead to amazing feats of stupidity when what is believed in isn't 100 percent good or 100 percent true. **BELIEF IN ANYTHING**

OTHER THAN WHAT, OR SHALL WE SAY WHO, IS 100 PERCENT GOOD AND 100 PERCENT TRUE WILL EVENTU- ALLY LEAD TO DISAPPOINTMENT, if not end in disaster.

That's because if the thing or person you believe in isn't perfect, then the thing or person will most defi- nitely disappoint in its moments of imperfection, and because of that, your bravery will lose its strength. But THE BRAVE WHO BASE THEIR COURAGE NOT ON THE IMPERFECT BUT ON THE PERFECT WILL NEVER BE DISAPPOINTED.

Where do you look for such perfection? Who or what can be trusted so completely that they can be given the title "perfect"? Though you may or may not believe it right now, there is a Perfect One, one who can be fully relied on by the Brave who look to him for courage. In him can be found all that is needed for perfect faith and perfect courage, because his very character confirms that NOTHING IN THIS LIFE IS BIGGER OR "BADDER" THAN HIM. NOTHING CAN SHAKE HIM OR ANYONE WHO BELIEVES IN HIM. HIS NAME IS GOD. In Deuteronomy 32:4 the Bible describes him like this: "He is a rock. What he does is perfect. All his ways are fair. He is a faithful God, who does no wrong. He is honorable and reliable." Reliable means you can put all your confidence in him without disappointment.

No shame comes to the person who believes in God enough to trust him (see Rom. 10:11). And that's the key: the belief must be strong enough to offer him complete trust in his character, which then translates to bravery.

A lot of people—you might even be one of them—have been disappointed by God. When God doesn't show up as hoped for; when trials come and pain lingers; when dreams die and plans are dashed to pieces, disappointment seems like the most obvious emotional response. But the person who truly trusts God doesn't translate their pain and suffering into doubt. That is, they are so completely convinced of who God is that they know that he can be trusted, even when things look bad.

In the amazing allegory *Hinds' Feet on High Places* by Hannah Hurnard, a little girl named Much-Afraid (because of her great fear and doubt) was going on a journey up the mountain with the Shepherd, who represents Jesus. As she began to freak out, the Shepherd asked her this question: "Would you be willing to trust me . . . even if everything in the wide world seemed to say that I was deceiving you—indeed, that I had deceived you all along?"

Her answer might shock you, but even in her fear she said this: "'Yes . . . I'm sure I would, because one

thing I know to be true, it is impossible that you should tell a lie. It is impossible that you should deceive me. I know that I am often very frightened at the things which you ask me to do,' she added shamefacedly and apologetically, 'but I could never doubt you in that way. It's myself I am afraid of, never of you, and though everyone in the world should tell me that you had deceived me, I should know it was impossible.'"[2]

It's easy to believe God when things are going well. It's logical. But when things start to go bad, that's when faith is put to the test. A lot of people fail the test of faith because they don't have enough faith for the hard and scary times. But those are exactly the times that faith is meant for, and the Brave understand that. Bravery is fed not by testosterone, alcohol, or sheer determination but by the power and the presence believed in and counted on—by the One who came to save us.

THE BIBLE IS PRETTY CLEAR THAT FAITH IS A RE-QUIREMENT FOR COURAGE. When the disciples were out on their little boat, caught in a storm, they freaked out and woke up Jesus, accusing him of not caring for them enough to wake up. In the midst of the turning and the tossing of the water they screamed, "Don't you care?" (Mark 4:38). Sound familiar? Have you ever wondered if God even cares? We all do at times, and it's not right, but it is human. These guys were scared to death, and his response to them was, "Why are you such cowards? Don't you have any faith yet?" (Mark 4:40). See the connection? Why are they cowards? Because they don't have faith. Faith is required for courage. Doubt leads to fear and worry and stress. Doubt destroys the Brave and makes them the scared.

Not only that, but this problem of not quite trusting God, of doubting his love and care for you, leads to a lack of blessing. When Jesus went home to Nazareth, the people had a hard time believing in him. They knew him as the kid down the block, not as the Son of God, and so they doubted him. It was unfortunate for them, because the Bible tells us that "because of their unbelief, he couldn't do any miracles among them except to place his hands on a few sick people and heal them. And he was amazed at their unbelief" (Mark 6:5–6 NLT). If your life needs a miracle and you can't find the courage to believe in the one who saves you, then your unbelief will be your own destruction. The Brave have the ability to trust God, especially when times get tough, and in that belief they just might find the bravery they were looking for in the form of a blessing. But even if they don't find a blessing, they are blessed just by the mere fact that they were overrun

with faith rather than fear, with confidence rather than doubt. Get this: bravery is your reward when you can believe all things good and perfect about God.

But if bravery hasn't been yours, have no fear. All you need is a better understanding of who God is. Knowing more about God allows you to put all of your confidence in him and removes the power of fear and doubt in your life. So let's take a look at the God of the Brave.

THE BRAVE KNOW GOD

The Brave have at least one thing in common, and that is their belief about who God is. The faith of the Brave isn't just about believing *in* God, though; it's about what you believe *about* God. It is essential to the brave in your life that you aren't believing a lie. **FEAR, THE KIND THAT CONTROLS YOU AND MAKES YOU SUFFER, IS EVIDENCE THAT YOU DON'T REALLY GET WHO GOD REALLY IS.** The Bible makes it clear: "No fear exists where his love is. Rather, perfect love gets rid of fear, because fear involves punishment. The person who lives in fear doesn't have perfect love" (1 John 4:18). The fear in your life comes from your inability to believe in God's perfect love, which might mean that you just don't fully know the character and the person of the God you so desperately want to believe in. That's natural; it happens all the time. We get mixed-up ideas of who God is because of the things that happen in our lives and the ways other human beings translate those things for us. If you've always been told a lie, it's really hard to see the truth. So before we go any further, we have to set down the foundation for the brave in your life, and that is the person of God. Who is he really? Can he be trusted to do and to be what he says he will do and be?

In order to answer these questions, **YOU HAVE TO UNDERSTAND THREE THINGS ABOUT GOD: HIS OMNIPOTENCE, HIS OMNISCIENCE, AND HIS OMNIPRESENCE.** These form the foundation of his character. They are big words that aren't used to describe anyone but God, so they don't get used a lot. Let's take a quick look at them.

First, **GOD IS OMNIPOTENT. THAT MEANS HE IS ALL-POWERFUL OR ALMIGHTY.** The Bible uses the word *almighty* 360 times to describe how powerful God is. No one else in heaven or on earth can be called almighty, having all power. In order to truly know God, you have to understand that he has all the power—all of it! There is nothing he can't do. Even if you feel like something in your life is more than he can handle, it's not, because nothing is more powerful than he is.

Second, **GOD IS OMNISCIENT OR ALL-KNOWING.** There is nothing you can inform him of or teach him, because he already knows everything (see Isa. 40:13–14). You aren't off his radar or out of his mind. You are always on his mind because he is all-knowing, which includes knowing what you are doing, thinking, and even feeling, all the time (read Ps. 139).

Third, **GOD IS OMNIPRESENT—HE IS EVERYWHERE.** This is good news. It means you are never alone but are always near the all-powerful and all-knowing God who loves you. Deuteronomy 31:6 is meant to make you brave when it says, "Be strong and courageous. Don't tremble! Don't be afraid of them! The LORD your God is the one who is going with you. He won't abandon you or leave you." When you feel like God is distant, gone, or not paying attention, that's a lie. The truth, confirmed by God's Word, is that he is everywhere, all the time. He cannot be distant or out of reach, or he wouldn't be everywhere; he'd only be most places.

These three attributes of God describe his power and his ability to do anything, know everything, and be everywhere at once. But all of this could be either really good news or horrific news, depending on how kind and loving God is. It's good if God's good, but it's bad, really bad, if God can't be trusted. A lot of us look at God that way. We think of him in human terms and assume he's bossy, manipulative, uncaring, distant, or angry. When you think of him like that, it's no wonder you are afraid. Who wouldn't be afraid of a God like that? But that is not the nature of God; it's the nature of fallen people. God cannot be known or judged by the hearts of broken human beings, stained with the residue of the sin in their lives. He has to be known by his Word. And his Word, the Bible, confirms an entirely different picture of God. In fact, the Bible confirms that God is the exact opposite of scary and distant when it says of him that he is love (1 John 4:8). A misunderstanding of this truth about who God is can lead to all kinds of emotional suffering and pain. If God isn't love, then look out, because all that power in the hands of a vindictive or bitter God would be disastrous for his children. But since God *is* love, we can know that there is no darkness in him.

Now, this doesn't mean that he's a sugar daddy who gives you everything you want whenever you want it, like a parent spoiling his child. That's not love; that's making stuff an idol. **AS THE PERFECT PARENT, GOD GIVES HIS CHILDREN WHAT THEY ASK FOR IF IT IS FOR THEIR GOOD, AND IF IT WOULD MEAN THEIR DESTRUCTION, HE WON'T GIVE IT TO THEM.** Like all good parents,

God actually disciplines those he loves (see Heb. 12:6). He doesn't abuse them, torture them, or shame them, but he protects them from unhealthy, sinful behavior so that they can be free from its bondage. His love produces all that is good in his children (see Phil. 2:13).

YOU HAVE TO BE CONVINCED THAT "LOVE" IS AN ACCURATE DESCRIPTION OF GOD IN ORDER TO FIND THE BRAVE IN YOUR LIFE. When your God is all-powerful and yet all-loving, then what do you fear? How can the child of such a perfect parent be in need? But wait, there's more: God can be trusted not only because of these things but also because he is

- wise, not stupid (Ps. 104:24)
- unchanging, not fickle (Heb. 1:12)
- faithful, not two-faced (1 Cor. 1:9)
- good, not bad (Ps. 25:8)
- just, not unfair (Rom. 2:6–16)
- merciful, not merciless (Luke 6:36)
- full of grace, not unforgiving (1 John 1:9)
- patient, not impatient (2 Pet. 3:9)
- holy, not imperfect (Exod. 15:11)

If God is all these things, it follows that you can trust that all he allows in your life is meant for your good. When you consider your life and God's role in it, you have to be willing to see him as sovereign—having absolute power to control everything. That means that **NOTHING THAT HAPPENS CATCHES GOD UNAWARE.** That means that **WHATEVER HE WANTS TO HAPPEN, HE WILL MAKE HAPPEN.** Even if you are suffering, he will not let the suffering be in vain. He uses all things together for the good of those who love him and have been called according to his plan (see Rom. 8:28).

FEAR HAS TO DO WITH DOUBT. When you fear, you doubt the character of God, and you believe a lie. It might be the lie that he won't come through, that he isn't involved, that he doesn't know what to do, or that he wants to hurt you. When you fear, you doubt God's goodness and "omni-ness," or "all-ness"—okay, maybe a better non-made-up word is *fullness*. When he becomes less than all to you, the fear takes over. But when you are confident in his sovereignty, nothing can push you around, control you, or destroy you. Nothing can move you from the feet of the Father (see Rom. 8:38–39), which is a place, by the way, of perfect rest and peace (see Isa. 26:3).

Listen, there are going to be hard times, no doubt. Jesus confirms it: "In the world you'll have trouble" (John 16:33). But what you think about those times and who you think they come from will either break you

or make you. If you can see that everything in the life of the believer comes first through the hands of God, then how can you fear? Take a look at Lamentations 3:38, which confirms this: "Both good and bad come from the mouth of the Most High God." How can you worry or doubt when you know that the most perfect being in the universe—the most loving, wise, and holy one—is actively and lovingly involved in every aspect of your life (see Prov. 16:9)? Every one! This means that even when things look bad, they are actually for your good. Sure, in this world you will have trouble, guaranteed, and that's where your faith gets shaky, because somewhere along the way you became convinced that faith meant a trouble-free life. That's not true. As it says in the book of John, the world comes with trouble, "But cheer up!" says Jesus. "I have overcome the world" (16:33). That means that it no longer feels like the world is against you when God is for you, because you see the world as just another tool in the hand of God. Though it might look like the world has the upper hand, it doesn't, because God has it all under control, the good and the bad. All of it comes from him (remember Lam. 3:38). And when all of it comes from him, that means no one else has control over your life or can destroy you. Even if the enemy should want to hurt you, he must first ask God's permission, as we see in the life of Job (see Job 1:6–12). This is freedom, and this is the foundation of all of your bravery. When you see God's hand rather than the enemy's, you are safe, even in the midst of destruction (see Job 13:15; Ps. 112:6–8; Prov. 3:25–26).

It's so important that you have a right-on view of the character and person of God. It's essential, because without it, all the trouble in this world will lead you to doubt, and then doubt will lead to worry, and worry will lead to panic, anger, depression, or hatred. All of your hope, any chance at being brave, lies in your ability to believe what is true about God and to take that with you into the battle of life. Without it there is no real and consistent bravery and no hope. So find out today who God is, and hold tight to that. He won't let you down. And then you can say, "The LORD is my light and my salvation. Who is there to fear? The LORD is my life's fortress. Who is there to be afraid of?" (Ps. 27:1).

THE BRAVE ARE CERTAIN OF WHAT THEY DON'T SEE

Your physical and emotional senses tell you all about the world around you. And when any or all of your

senses warn you danger is near, it's natural to react by either fighting or running. Your heartbeat races, your body sweats, your face gets flushed, and your mouth gets dry, all in response to your sense that something is wrong. But as a believer you have another aspect to your senses, and that is the sense of your spirit or, more accurately, Christ's Spirit within you. With this spiritual sense you can override a lot of your physical and emotional senses with the calm truth that you can do all things through Christ who strengthens you (see Phil. 4:13). Knowing that there is a world around you that can't be seen with human eyes, where the Spirit is fighting for you and surrounding you with protection, is an essential part of the mind and spirit of the Brave who are sure of what they hope for and certain of what they do not see (see Heb. 11:1).

YOU CANNOT SEE THE HAND OF GOD IN YOUR LIFE WITH YOUR PHYSICAL EYES, BUT IT IS THERE (see Isa. 41:10). You cannot see the angel that God has sent to protect you, but he is there (see Pss. 34:7; 91:11). You cannot see the future, but you can be sure that God can and that he has plans for you, plans to prosper you and not to harm you (see Jer. 29:11).

Faith, and therefore **BRAVERY, IS NOT ABOUT WHAT YOU SEE OR FEEL AROUND YOU BUT ABOUT WHAT YOU**

BELIEVE TO BE TRUE IN SPITE OF WHAT YOU SEE AND FEEL. In this life you will have trouble, and you can't let that trouble either define you or control you, but you have to live by faith—faith that sees beyond the physical, into the spiritual, with all truth and wisdom. God's Word confirms the courage that comes from this way of life when Paul says, "So we are always of good courage" because "we walk by faith, not by sight" (2 Cor. 5:6–7 ESV).

THE BRAVE LET GOD DO THE WORK

Being certain of what they do not see, the Brave are able to be fully convinced of the presence of God at all times. Not only that, but **THE BRAVE KNOW THAT IT ISN'T BY THEIR OWN STRENGTH OR MIGHT THAT THEY DO ANYTHING, BUT IT'S ONLY THROUGH THE SPIRIT OF GOD THAT LIVES INSIDE OF THEM** (see Zech. 4:6). Knowing where all the power to fight fear, worry, sin, and all the other bad and oppressive things in your life comes from is a major step toward becoming one of the Brave. When life threatens to get the best of you and everything around you is chaos, God has something to say about it. "Do not be afraid!" he says (2 Chron. 20:15 NLT). This isn't just a suggestion or a positive

I KNOW THE PLANS THAT I HAVE FOR YOU, DECLARES THE LORD.

THEY ARE PLANS FOR PEACE AND NOT DISASTER, PLANS TO GIVE YOU A FUTURE FILLED WITH HOPE.

JEREMIAH 29:11

mantra to repeat in order to feel better. This is a command, and one that comes with an exclamation point for emphasis. If it's a command, that means it can be done! Reversing fear has to be possible, or it would be insanity to command people to do it. The next part of the verse explains how to defeat your fear when the enemy attacks: "Don't be discouraged by this mighty army, for the battle is not yours, but God's."

When a "mighty army" stands up against you, either figuratively or literally, it can feel like it's all on you to defend yourself, but this verse says nope, that's not true. **WHEN THE WORLD ATTACKS, THE BATTLE IS NOT YOURS BUT GOD'S.** And furthermore, if it's his, then he will fight it for you. That's the good news surrounding the commands of God. When something is commanded, you can be sure that you can do it, because you don't do any of it alone but with the help and the power of the Holy Spirit. In fact, the weaker you are, the stronger he is. Paul found this out when he had something bad in his life that just wouldn't go away. God told him, "My grace is sufficient for you, for my power is made perfect in weakness" (2 Cor. 12:9 ESV).

The battle that the Brave fight isn't fought alone; in fact, it isn't really even fought by the Brave but is fought by the God in whom the Brave put all their confidence.

Your weakness doesn't matter. All you have to do is have enough strength to believe.

THE BRAVE ACCEPT GOD'S PROTECTION

God wants you to know that you don't go into battle alone. When bullets fly and the flaming arrows of criticism or temptation start to zoom toward your head, you aren't unprotected, unless you choose not to put on the armor that God offers you. Ephesians 6 lays out the believer's spiritual armor, and part of that armor is a shield. The shield protects your core—your heart, your lungs, the important organs of your body—so it is very important. This shield is called the shield of faith, and you are told to "hold up the shield of faith to stop the fiery arrows of the devil" (Eph. 6:16 NLT). When you drop the shield, you lose faith and doubt takes over. Then nothing is blocking those fiery arrows of the devil from getting to your heart. That's a poetic way of saying that **WHEN YOU START TO DOUBT THE PROVIDENCE AND THE SOVEREIGNTY OF GOD, YOUR HEART BECOMES OPEN TO LIES**—lies that are meant to distort your idea of the true character of God. These lies, once believed, wreak havoc on the life of faith and on the believer's ability to be brave. Remember, **BRAVERY CAN'T EXIST**

TRUST IN THE *Lord* AND DO GOOD.

THEN YOU WILL LIVE SAFELY IN THE LAND AND PROSPER.

TAKE DELIGHT IN THE *LORD*,

AND HE WILL GIVE YOU
YOUR HEART'S DESIRES.

COMMIT EVERYTHING YOU
DO TO THE *LORD*.

TRUST HIM, AND HE WILL
HELP YOU.

PSALM 37:3-5 NLT

WITHOUT FAITH. So if you lack the faith you wish you had, you can find it when you use the truth to block the lies that come at you.

WHEN YOU START TO BELIEVE SOMETHING THAT IS INCONSISTENT WITH WHO GOD IS, THAT'S THE BEGINNING OF YOUR DESTRUCTION. In the Garden of Eden, the serpent helped Eve convince herself that God was a liar. He said that God wasn't being honest when he said that if she ate the fruit from the tree of the knowledge of good and evil, she would surely die (see Gen. 3:1–5). This lie about the character of God convinced Eve that eating the fruit was the best option, and as a result the world was introduced to sin, which would lead to the separation of humanity from God and all our troubles since that introduction. When you don't take up the shield of faith to stop the lies from taking hold of your heart, sin takes over, and sin (not doing what God commands or doing what God forbids) plants the seeds of fear in your heart. This fear comes from both concern over your guilt (see 1 John 4:18) and doubt of God's goodness. Sin is taking life into your own hands and not accepting the protection of God in the form of the shield of faith, which he offers to help you fight against the lies that convince you of God's lack of care in your life and that lead you to step in and take over for him.

THE BRAVE KNOW ANYTHING IS POSSIBLE

> Jesus said to him, "As far as possibilities go, everything is possible for the person who believes. (Mark 9:23)

THE AMAZING THING ABOUT THE BRAVE IS THAT THEY THINK THAT THINGS OTHER PEOPLE SAY CAN NEVER HAPPEN ARE POSSIBLE. They have hope that shines like the noonday sun. They are comfortable in chaos because they have an unwavering faith that it will all work out for good. *IT'S NOT THAT THEY ARE CONFIDENT THAT MIRACLES WILL BE THE ANSWER TO ALL THEIR PRAYERS BUT THAT THEY ARE COMFORTABLE WITH THE IDEA THAT EVEN IF THE MIRACLE DOESN'T COME, LIFE IS STILL GOOD, BECAUSE THE MIRACLE WAS NOT GOD'S BEST FOR THEM.* When you complain or whine about life, fear the worst, and work with all your might to avoid what you think will be your certain destruction, you accuse God of being either not as good as he ought to be or not as influential as he could be. But for the person who never doubts the character of God, it's possible to believe that even a disaster could be God's best. Job understood this when he said, "Though he slay me, I will hope in him" (Job 13:15 ESV).

Yes, **THE BRAVE KNOW ANYTHING IS POSSIBLE, EX-CEPT THAT GOD WOULD EVER FAIL, LEAVE, OR GIVE UP.** They know that with faith, all is not only survivable but beautiful. And they can find the courage to be brave not because of who they are but because of who God is.

THE BRAVE ARE SAFE

> A person's fear sets a trap for him,
> but one who trusts the LORD is safe.
> (Proverbs 29:25)

How can your trust in God lead to safety? How can you say that you are safe when you are being attacked, abused, or hated? Where is the safety in that? The safety is found not in the removal of the attacks from your life but in the removal of the fear from your life. When others sin, you can't do much to stop them. Everyone makes their own choices, and outside of physically restraining them, controlling another human being is almost impossible. The sin in others confirms what God's Word says: "There is no one righteous, not even one" (Rom. 3:10 NIV).

In a world where others around you sin, sometimes horribly, how can you claim the safety of God? While God has saved many of his children from terrible fates, many others have had to suffer greatly. Just look at the disciples. All but John were killed in a gruesome way for not disowning Christ. These saints looked for something more important than the safety of their bodies: the safety of their souls. They knew that eternity waits for the soul that doesn't lose faith. And as Paul says,

> Our suffering is light and temporary and is producing for us an eternal glory that is greater than anything we can imagine. We don't look for things that can be seen but for things that can't be seen. Things that can be seen are only temporary. But things that can't be seen last forever. (2 Cor. 4:17–18)

Fear sets a trap for your soul, because it deceives the soul into moving from faith to doubt. And when that happens you easily find yourself confused and alone. But when you stay convinced that God is all good, then no matter what might happen around you, you will still have faith, and you will be able to say these words that will encourage not only you but anyone else who listens:

> *God is our refuge and strength,*
>   *an ever-present help in times of trouble.*
> *That is why we are not afraid*
>   *even when the earth quakes*

or the mountains topple into the
depths of the sea.
Water roars and foams,
and mountains shake at the
surging waves. (Ps. 46:1–3)

Notice it doesn't say that the earth won't quake if you believe or that the mountains won't topple. No, it says that **ALL THESE TERRIBLE THINGS MIGHT TAKE PLACE, BUT THE PEOPLE WHO TRUST GOD WILL BE SAFE, NO MATTER WHAT MIGHT HAPPEN TO THEIR BODIES.**

As we've seen, the Brave all have one thing in common: faith. They all believe in a God who is not only good and powerful but also perfect in all he does. They have such a secure faith in who he is that nothing can topple them and nothing can truly hurt them. The world will still try. Mountains will still crumble, but the heart of the Brave will remain intact. All of this rests not on who they are but on who God is and what he has done in their lives. The Brave live by the power of the Holy Spirit within them that teaches them, counsels them, and guides them into the truth that sets them free from the fears of this world—free to believe, to love, and to hope.

If your faith is weak and you don't feel that power yet, don't let that be a reason to fear, but choose to hope. God has brought you to these pages for a reason. He has not left you alone in your misery. He is actively pursuing you, showing you his character and his desire to be all that you need. Take this chance to thank him, to confess your doubt to him, and to promise to find out who he really is and begin to believe in the goodness of who he is. Ask him for help, and he will give it. May today be for you the beginning of a new life and a new ability to become a part of the Brave.

Girls, have more conversation about *THE BRAVE* at **GodGirl.com**!

Guys, have more conversation about *THE BRAVE* at **GodGuy.com**!

CHAPTER

2

THE BRAVE

FEAR THE
RIGHT THING

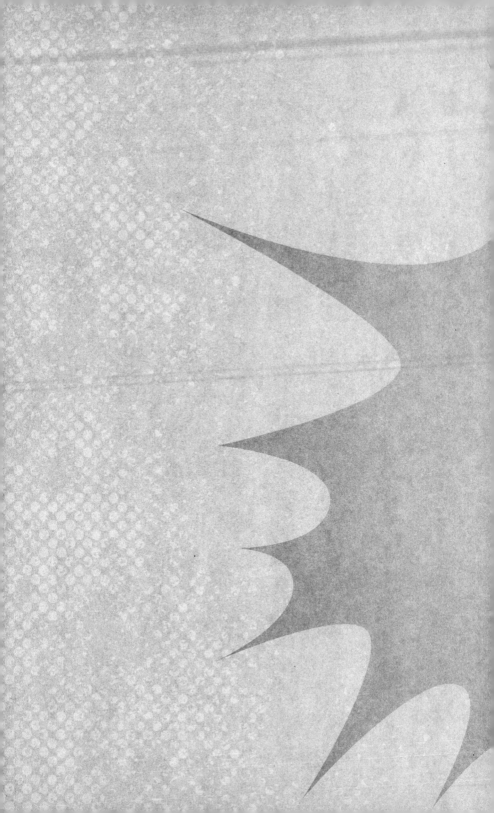

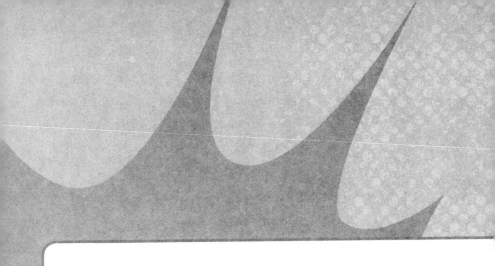

BRAVERY DOESN'T HAPPEN IN THE ABSENCE OF FEAR. That's because there has to be fear in order for there to be courage and in order for the brave to exist. You wouldn't say, "I was so brave to hold that puppy!" or "It took a lot of courage to eat that piece of chocolate cake." No fear, no bravery. It is because of the fearful things in life that the Brave even need to exist. So if you have fear, then you have been given the chance to be brave. The long-dead American general George Patton is often quoted as saying, "If we take the generally accepted definition of bravery as a quality which knows no fear, I have never seen a brave man. All men are frightened. The more intelligent they are, the more they are frightened." See, it's the frightening nature of something that lays the foundation for bravery. So in any discussion of the idea of the Brave, we have to know bravery's source: fear.

FEAR IS AN IMPORTANT PART OF LIFE. Most people don't like it and don't want it, but we all have it. Somewhere deep down you have things that you fear, no question. **WHAT YOU FEAR SAYS A LOT ABOUT YOU.** In fact, your fears can explain your faith. People who don't fear God have no faith. People who fear other people don't fear God enough. **FEAR IS A GOOD GAUGE OF FAITH.** So let's look deeper into the face of fear and see if that doesn't help the brave in your life to grow.

GOOD FEAR, BAD FEAR

First of all, you have to know that **NOT ALL FEAR IS BAD.** There is good fear and bad fear; fear to be obeyed and fear to fight against. **GOOD FEAR LEADS YOU TO DO THINGS THAT ARE GOOD AND HEALTHY,** things that serve God and lead you away from danger and toward safety. Good fear says, "There's a hurricane coming and people are being evacuated, so I'm gonna get in the car and go." Good fear says, "It is a dreadful thing to fall into the hands of the living God" (Heb. 10:31 NIV). **GOOD FEAR PROTECTS YOU FROM DESTRUCTION** and keeps your fears from becoming reality. This kind of fear needs to be responded to with an action that does something about it. This is a saving kind of fear. In fact, it's the fear of God himself that leads people to confess that they have gotten life all wrong and to realize that they have sinned. That fear of God's punishment for sin—fear of life forever separated from him—leads to the most important event in a human's life: their salvation.

You can't categorically say that fear is bad and that you want nothing to do with it, because there are a lot of fearful things that are fearful for a reason. In these cases **BRAVERY OVER GOOD FEAR WOULD BE INSANE.** To say "I'm brave! I can go pet that alligator" is crazy and stupid. Some fearful things exist in order to serve you and your faith.

This is why good fears and bad fears get all muddled: because the bad fears promise to do the same thing for you. They promise to protect you from whatever you fear. Maybe you fear rejection, failure, dangers that are out of your control, or never finding love. Maybe you're afraid of not pleasing others and what they might do to you. These kinds of fears pretend to be good fears, set in place for your own protection. Like the fear of leaving your house to avoid getting in a terrible accident, they claim to be for your own safety. But what these fears also bring is a life in a prison of your own making, shackled with worry and the sin that is required to keep those fears from becoming a reality.

WHEN FEAR LEADS TO A SINFUL ACTION, THEN YOU'VE GOT A PROBLEM. It's like this: you are afraid of not being liked, so you lie about something in order to impress someone, and your fear of not being liked trumps your fear of God and your obedience to his command not to lie. When your fear of losing your loved ones in a freak car accident leads you to worry every time they get into a car, you choose trusting your fear over trusting your God. So the key to bravery isn't getting rid of the fear but fearing the right thing.

To sum it up, **GOOD FEAR LEADS YOU CLOSER TO GOD, WHILE BAD FEAR LEADS YOU AWAY FROM GOD AND TOWARD SIN.** Fear will always be a part of our human condition. We will always have opportunities to fear for ourselves and for others, but that doesn't mean that fear has to control us. Fear can be controlled, surrendered, and used for good when we quickly distinguish between good fear and bad fear.

THE BRAVE FEAR GOD

THE MOST IMPORTANT GOOD FEAR IS THE FEAR OF GOD. Proverbs 1:7 says, "The fear of the LORD is the beginning of knowledge." That means **THE FEAR OF GOD IS A HEALTHY FEAR,** because it brings knowledge, and with knowledge comes a bunch of other amazing things like wisdom, hope, peace, rest, love, and joy. **TO STAND UP IN THE FACE OF THE FEAR OF GOD ISN'T BRAVERY; IT'S STUPIDITY.** The people who reject the fear of God are rejecting God himself, because their taming of his awesome power makes him no longer God but "the big guy upstairs" or "my buddy God." A lack of fear leads to a lack of reverence and awe. How can you bow down to and worship one whose power isn't big enough to fear?

A HEALTHY FEAR OF GOD DOESN'T LEAD TO SIN. It doesn't make you worry, stress, fear for your safety, or doubt his love, kindness, grace, or forgiveness. That would be the fear of a god with human attributes. If God were vindictive, evil, unforgiving, and unloving, then yes, you should fear him like you fear an abusive father. But knowing that God is love and that his very nature can't be separated from his attributes of kindness, mercy, grace, and righteousness, you have to know that the fear of God that is the beginning of knowledge is a healthy fear. **IT'S NOT A FEAR OF THE UNPREDICTABILITY AND VOLATILITY OF GOD BUT OF THE AWESOMENESS AND HOLINESS OF GOD.** When you can conceive of such a powerful being reaching down and loving you, giving you not only your life but the life of his Son as

well, then your fear is less a fear of his wrath and more a fear of hurting him or disappointing him.

When Hayley was growing up, she never got into trouble. It wasn't because she was afraid of the punishment of her dad but because she was afraid of disappointing him, of hurting him. She wanted so badly to please him, because she loved and admired him so, and the "fear" of failing at that is what compelled her to obedience and respect, not the fear of his anger or temper. The same is true with God. When you fear not loving him as he deserves rather than fearing his wrath or violence, then you fear God properly.

THE FEAR OF GOD COMES FROM A CORRECT UNDERSTANDING NOT OF GOD'S UNPREDICTABILITY BUT OF THE ABSOLUTE PREDICTABILITY OF HIS UNWAVERING LOVE, grace, generosity, mercy, and kindness and an understanding of his hatred of all things sinful. When you understand what pleases God and what angers him, then you prefer the former over the latter. A real understanding of the nature of God's holiness and his desire for holiness in the lives of those who love him produces the fear of God in your life.

THIS FEAR OF GOD—OF HURTING HIM, OF DISAPPOINTING HIM—IS A FEAR THAT COMPELS YOU TO RIGHTEOUSNESS. In other words, it makes you want to do right, to be good, to obey God's Word. When you take God at his word, you are bound to feel a real fear of disagreeing with him, of turning to sin, of choosing to reject his commands and his teachings. The writer of Psalm 119 understood that fear when he said, "My body shudders in fear of you, and I am afraid of your regulations" (v. 120). Peter puts it this way: "If you call God your Father, live your time as temporary residents on earth in fear. He is the God who judges all people by what they have done, and he doesn't play favorites" (1 Pet. 1:17).

This fear of God shouldn't freak you out and scare you but should drive you to stand in awe, to worship his greatness, and to fear not his wrath, because that has been taken up by the death of Christ on the cross, but being separated from him by disbelief. The failure to fear him as God is what should be feared. The Brave don't reject the fear of God but embrace it as fuel for the bravery they need in the rest of life.

THE BRAVE RESPECT DANGER

ANOTHER KIND OF FEAR THAT DOESN'T NEED TO BE OVERCOME BY THE BRAVE IS A FEAR OF REAL DANGER. This kind of fear needs to be listened to, because its goal

is to lead you to safety, protect you, and even save your life. For example, the fear of being burned is a good fear when you are in a home that is on fire. Knowing what to fear—the fire, in this case—will protect you from harm. Good fear doesn't need bravery; it needs quick and decisive action. No one sees fire climbing up the walls and has to think about whether they are going to get out or not. The fear compels you to action. So good fear leads you to good actions.

Some Christians take the position that having no fear is good, so when danger comes, they refuse it. They claim they don't need things that other people need, because God has them covered. While that is true to some extent, it isn't true in all cases.

Have you heard the story of the man who was caught in a flood? As the waters rose, he refused to fear. When the water came to his front door, some men came by in wading boots and said, "It's time to go, the water is rising." But the man just said, "God will save me. I'm going to wait on him." So the men left. Then the waters pushed the man up to the second floor of his house. As he hung out the window, some people came by in a boat and said, "Get in! It isn't safe in there. We're here to help you." But the man said, "No, that's okay. I'm trusting God. He'll save me." So the people left. The water continued to rise as predicted, and the man had to make a hole in his roof and crawl out on top. As he stood teetering on his rooftop, a helicopter came by and lowered a lifeline. The man looked up and said, "No, thank you. I'm waiting on God to save me." Not long after that, the water rose and covered the man's house, and soon he found himself in a river of rushing water. Unable to stay afloat, the man drowned. When he got to heaven, he asked God, "Why didn't you save me? I trusted you!" God looked at him and shook his head. "I sent you some men in boots to take you to safety, but you refused. Then I sent you a boat, but you rejected that. Finally I sent a helicopter, but you wouldn't take the help I sent."

SOMETIMES GOD SENDS DANGEROUS AND FEARFUL THINGS THAT ARE MEANT TO BE RUN FROM, NOT STOOD UP TO. The warning of real danger might just be God's way of saving you, but you'll never receive that if you don't heed the warning. The Old Testament is full of cases where disaster was coming and God's people were told to get out. When God was set to destroy Sodom and Gomorrah, he told Lot and his family to get out (see Gen. 19:12–29). It would have been silly for them to say, "No, we'll be brave and stay. No fear!" when God had told them to get up and get going

because the end was coming. And while God doesn't tell us directly to get out when danger is imminent, like he did in the days of the prophets, he does send others to notify us of real danger. So when the StormTracker 3000 says the tornado is headed for your house, don't stand up and bravely defy it, but take cover. Pray, of course. Trust God, yes. Don't worry, definitely! But don't be stupidly brave in the face of real danger. Avoid the stupid bravery Satan tempted Jesus with when he told him to jump off of the tall temple, knowing that the angels would save him (see Matt. 4:5–7). The fear of God requires that we fear him enough to protect the temple of the Holy Spirit, which is our bodies (see 1 Cor. 6:19). Being a fool by ignoring the warning signs is stupid bravery.

THE BRAVE DON'T FEAR PEOPLE

One of the most common fears in the world is the fear of people—not just what people might do to you but also what people might *think* about you. You're fearing people when you get stressed out about what people think about you or when you make decisions and do things because you don't want someone to dislike you or hate you. You also do things out of this fear when you imagine that your value or worth is based on what other people think about you rather than on what God knows about you. This is nothing new. John 12:42–43 says, "Many rulers believed in Jesus. However, they wouldn't admit it publicly because the Pharisees would have thrown them out of the synagogue. They were more concerned about what people thought of them than about what God thought of them." Fearing the disapproval of people more than you fear the disapproval of God is just as much a tragedy now as it was back then.

Fearing people is an easy trap to fall into because you are surrounded by them almost continually. You can see their faces when they are mad or judgmental; you can hear their voices and see their actions. In a lot of ways, they can feel more real (and seem more important) than God, and that's why it's so easy to start to fall into worrying about what they think. But how exhausting it is trying to please people! And how dangerous!

It was the fear of not pleasing people that caused Michael the most pain in his life, to the point that he never ended up pleasing people. He just hurt them by not ever telling them the truth but only saying what he thought they wanted to hear. Michael's constant reminder to escape this lifelong fear is Galatians 1:10:

"For am I now seeking the approval of man, or of God? Or am I trying to please man? If I were still trying to please man, I would not be a servant of Christ" (ESV).

Bravery is called for in order to save you from your fear of people. When tempted to obsess over what another human thinks, **THE BRAVE REMEMBER WHO THEY LIVE TO PLEASE, AND THEY RUN EVERYTHING THROUGH THAT FILTER.** If they feel an urge to please another human, they check that urge against God's Word. Is what I'm compelled to do a commandment? Does it fit into "Turn your other cheek" (Matt. 5:39) or "If someone forces you to go one mile, go two miles with him" (Matt. 5:41)? Or am I trying to please this person so he or she won't hate me, will do what I want, or will continue to love me? The list goes on and on. It's all about motive. When you want to please someone, ask yourself why. The answer will help you figure out if it's something you ought to do or not. When the motive is all about you—your status, your feelings, your fears—then it's not a holy, God-honoring motive. **FEARING MAKING OTHER PEOPLE UPSET BECAUSE OF HOW THAT WILL AFFECT YOU ISN'T HUMILITY BUT PRIDE.**

THE BRAVE DO WHAT IS RIGHT, EVEN IF IT MIGHT MAKE OTHER PEOPLE MAD OR UNCOMFORTABLE. They try to do it in a loving way, but they don't let something like discomfort keep them from obeying God. That's really what it's about: your fear of discomfort. It's uncomfortable to be disliked, judged, or thought poorly of in any way. For a lot of people pleasers, the idea of not making people happy by giving them whatever they want sounds terribly uncomfortable. *THE FEAR OF PEOPLE AND A LACK OF FAITH TO STAND UP FOR WHAT IS RIGHT, NOBLE, AND GOOD COMES FROM WHAT YOU WORSHIP THE MOST: YOUR OWN COMFORT.*

THE BRAVE WILL RISK DISCOMFORT TO PLEASE GOD OVER SELF. They risk things like the discomfort of not living up to others' expectations in order to do what God commands. This kind of bravery shows up when you don't do what the world expects, when you don't look for glory or fame, when your goal isn't being better than others or being loved but loving others more than yourself (see Phil. 2:3).

THE BRAVE KNOW WHAT CAN'T BE CONTROLLED

There are a lot of things to fear in this world. A lot of fears can protect you from danger, but even more can put you *in* danger. The fear of being consumed by something you cannot control is one of those dangerous

fears. Fearing the things you have no control over is like getting on a stationary bike to try to pedal to safety. It's all sweat and no distance. If you can't control something, like natural disasters or finding love, then worrying about it, fearing it, or being consumed by it is all spin and no progress.

The Brave know what can't be controlled, and they let all of it go. They can let it go for two reasons. The first is that they know that even if they can't control it, there is still someone who can (and is). The second is that they know that if whatever they fear should come to pass, it would be for the best, because of that someone who is in control. The sovereignty of God, the fact that all things are under his control and that nothing happens unless he directs it or allows it, makes the Brave able to be brave because they leave nothing to chance but everything to God, trusting that he has it all under control. In Ephesians 1:11 we read that God "works all things according to the counsel of his will" (ESV). Did you get that? "All things," not just some things. Sovereignty means God doesn't just have the right or the power to rule over all things but that he *always does* rule all things, without exception. And if he has it all under control, then anything believers might suffer would be only what is best for them.

The life of the apostle Paul was filled with hundreds of things he couldn't control. Just read a small clip of the story of his life:

> [I faced] imprisonments, with countless beatings, and often near death. Five times I received at the hands of the Jews the forty lashes less one. Three times I was beaten with rods. Once I was stoned. Three times I was shipwrecked; a night and a day I was adrift at sea; on frequent journeys, in danger from rivers, danger from robbers, danger from my own people, danger from Gentiles, danger in the city, danger in the wilderness, danger at sea, danger from false brothers; in toil and hardship, through many a sleepless night, in hunger and thirst, often without food, in cold and exposure. (2 Cor. 11:23–27 ESV)

He couldn't control the whip that struck his back, the stones that hit his body, the waves that wrecked his ship, the robbers that threatened his possessions, or the wild animals that threatened his life. But look what he said about his shipwrecked and tattered life: "I consider our present sufferings insignificant compared to the glory that will soon be revealed to us" (Rom. 8:18).

Paul was certain that even when God let just about everything be taken away from him, it was nothing compared with what God would give him in return—eternal

life, as in forever and ever and ever. Paul trusted God with the scary and hard parts of life, knowing that a life turned over to him would never be a disappointment, no matter what it looked like on the outside. He knew he was part of a story bigger than his own, one that would change the world. Because of that and because of his determination to serve the living God, he didn't wimp out. He didn't worry, or fear, or turn tail and run. He taught the Brave the meaning of bravery.

Knowing that God can be trusted not only with eternity but also with today, with this very second in time, will open your life to the brave that you've always wanted. **IF GOD CAN SAVE YOUR LIFE FOR ETERNITY, THEN YOU MUST BELIEVE THAT HE CAN SAVE YOUR LIFE FOR TODAY.** The brave that is enduring is the brave that is founded in the power and the presence of an all-knowing and loving God and in knowing that what is out of your control is well within his.

WHEN YOU THINK ABOUT IT, FEAR ALL COMES DOWN TO THIS: CONTROL. There are a lot of things in your life that you can't control. You can't control other people. You can't control your friends or family. You can't control the weather, disasters, or accidents. You can't control what the doctors do or don't do to you while you are in surgery. You can't control the fact that you are going to die one day. There are a ton of things you can't control—that's life. The problem comes when that feeling of being out of control scares you. That's when you let fear take over, and brave walks out the door. If you have no control over something, then fearing it is useless. When Hayley was younger (like last year, ha!), she had a huge fear of tornadoes. Living in Tennessee means we see a lot of them. She would freak out every time the news said "Tornado Watch." But when she concentrated on the fact that her fear didn't help the situation, that it didn't divert the storm or protect her or our family, and that only God could change the weather, she loosened up a little bit and found the brave she needed not to freak out.

FEARING WHAT YOU CAN'T CONTROL IS A WASTE OF ENERGY. It serves no purpose other than to stress you out and make you sick. This kind of fear says to God, "I don't trust you with things I can't control," and it's a bad fear. Being brave in those situations is refusing to let fear rule your heart. It's refusing to let it control you. Being brave means saying no to the fear of things you can't control because you accept that you can't control them. **FEAR TELLS YOU THE LIE THAT IF YOU**

FEAR THE SITUATION ENOUGH, YOU CAN HAVE SOME KIND OF CONTROL OVER IT, but fear isn't a step in the direction of being in control—it's a step toward being even more out of control.

Fearing the wrong things makes the Brave not so brave. But bravery can be yours if you will put your fears into perspective. **FEARING GOD OVER PEOPLE IS THE FOUNDATION OF BEING BRAVE.** Don't get your fears mixed up and obey the bad fears, ones that need to be disobeyed, while ignoring the good ones that are meant to protect you. Fear is a normal part of life; it's what you do with it that will make or break you. Fear is bad when it leads you to sin instead of faith. **WHEN FEAR DRIVES YOU AWAY FROM GOD, YOU HAVE A PROBLEM,** but when it drives you to his feet, then you have found the brave you were looking for.

CHAPTER 3

KNOW THE
TRUTH

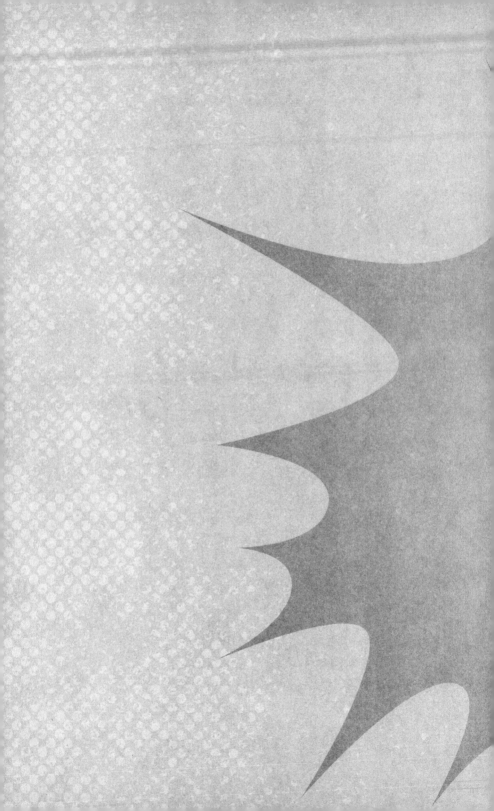

YOU WILL KNOW THE TRUTH, AND THE TRUTH WILL SET YOU FREE" (JOHN 8:32 ESV). Have you ever heard that expression? How can truth set you free? What does it set you free from? Truth sets you free from worry, fear, and doubt, because the truth is that God is still God no matter what might happen to or around you. The truth is that God can be trusted and that the Brave can do whatever he would have them do, no matter what the consequences or how severe the pain.

Truth is essential to faith and to the brave in your life. **WITHOUT TRUTH, FAITH IS INSANITY.** Believing a lie and hoping that it will somehow prove to be true is crazy. But the truth found in God's Word sets you free from being enslaved in lies. The Bible calls Satan "the father of lies" (John 8:44). That means he gave birth to lying, and he uses lies to further his kingdom. But the truth is victorious over his lies.

He cannot stand against truth. He is defeated by it. When Satan took Jesus to the wilderness to tempt him, Jesus responded to all of Satan's lies with truth, and that truth he spoke destroyed all of Satan's schemes, and he had to give up and leave. The same is true for you: *LIES DESTROY LIFE, BUT TRUTH SETS YOU FREE FROM THE BONDAGE TO SIN THAT THREATENS TO DESTROY YOUR LIFE AND THE LIVES OF THOSE AROUND YOU.*

THE BRAVE RESPOND TO LIES WITH THE TRUTH. They can do that because they know the truth so well. It is essential to the brave in you that you know the truth so you can act upon it. Even if your present truth is pain and suffering, your future truth is an eternity with the Father, and that is all the power that brave needs to survive in you. So let's take a look at the truth that will set you free to become a part of the Brave.

THE BRAVE KNOW THE WILL OF GOD IS BETTER THAN THEIR OWN

The human will is powerful. What you want—what you really, really want—can be the most preoccupying, self-absorbing, time-consuming, obsessing, and exhausting stuff in your life. *A WILL SET ON*

SOMETHING IT CAN'T HAVE, HAS LOST, OR FEARS LOS-ING IS STRESSED OUT AND MISERABLE. This is how it starts: You want (or you "will") something, and your mind starts to imagine what it will be like to have that something. Then your heart takes over and falls in love with that something, dreaming about it all the time, imagining holding it or living it or whatever. Soon your will is doing all it can to get whatever it is that it wants, and it stops at just about nothing to get it.

The result is a life that loses focus; it starts to be all about the lack of what it wants instead of the abundance of what it has. Discontentment sets in, and the will can go one of two directions.

One, it can become aggressive and fight harder for what it wants, ignoring all the pain, suffering, or loss that it might encounter. You can see this in the life of the addict, who ignores all the red flags and warning signs and keeps on after the prize that he has set his eyes on.

Two, the will can become resigned, believing the dream will never come true and living in sadness, doubt, fear, and even depression over what the person so terribly wants but never will get.

A lot of people throughout time have given themselves completely over to their wills and have preferred

them to the very will of God. They have chosen lust over love, doubt over belief, and fear over faith. But the power of the Brave is in their knowledge that the will of God is far better than their own, because their will, or desire, can make them feel good while being at best unproductive and at worst totally destructive.

The life of Christ gives us the perfect example of a life set on the will of God over the will of self. While he was on earth, Jesus was 100 percent human and 100 percent God. That means that while he was always God, he was also completely human, feeling the same things we humans feel, experiencing our pain, living in our mixed-up world, and having to deal with all that goes with that. He knew what mean people were like. He knew how their words cut and their clubs wounded. He knew how it felt to be rejected, to be ignored, to be hated. He had desires that threatened to consume him, emotions that wanted to overtake him. He loved, he hurt, he cried (see John 11:5, 33, 35). And when he was in the worst possible anguish a human could ever be in, when he was preparing for the cross, he said to his Father, "If you are willing, remove this cup from me. Nevertheless, not my will, but yours, be done" (Luke 22:42 ESV). He had a will—it was not to suffer the death of the crucifixion—but *HIS WILL NEVER TRUMPED*

THE WILL OF THE FATHER, and so he didn't disappear when they came for him and didn't come down from the cross, because he knew that God's will, no matter how painful, is perfect.

A lot of people might think Jesus could do all that because of his divine nature. But he didn't use his heavenly powers to overcome the pain of the cross. He had to deal with the torture and crucifixion as a 100 percent human man, setting aside the power that comes with being 100 percent God. That means **HE <u>CHOSE</u> TO ENDURE THE WORST POSSIBLE PAIN WITHOUT CALLING ON HIS DIVINE POWERS.** Instead of calling on what was a natural part of his attributes, he called and relied on the Father. That's good news—it means that **THE BRAVE YOU SEE IN THE LIFE OF CHRIST IS THE SAME BRAVE YOU CAN HAVE.** You don't have to be the Son of God to endure, to rise above, and to live through the suffering of this life. Take a look at what 1 Peter 2:21 says about how your life will resemble Christ's when it comes to the brave in you: "God called you to endure suffering because Christ suffered for you. He left you an example so that you could follow in his footsteps." The Brave don't fear any amount of suffering. Like Christ, they trust the Father, so they are bent on enduring whatever might come

their way, trusting that God has it all under control and all within his plan. This same passage in 1 Peter goes on to tell us a little bit about how Christ acted on that terrible day and by extension how you are called to act when trials and suffering tempt you to fear and to doubt: "Christ never committed any sin. He never spoke deceitfully. Christ never verbally abused those who verbally abused him. When he suffered, he didn't make any threats" (vv. 22–23). How did he do it? How was he so brave in the face of such persecution, torture, and bullying? He "left everything to the one who judges fairly" (v. 23).

In times of testing, in fearful and treacherous situations, when bad people attack and life threatens to get the best of them, the Brave remember one thing: they remember the One who judges fairly. That means even though their hearts want to scream out, "This isn't fair!" they declare "He *is* fair." They trust the justice of the Father.

THE BRAVE KNOW HE WORKS ALL THINGS TOGETHER FOR GOOD

Imagine you knew the future. Imagine you knew what would happen tomorrow and the next day, and you

THE BRAVE KNOW THE TRUTH

knew it would be good. Sure, you might know that you would live through a terrible storm and almost lose your life. You might know that you would lose someone you love very much and be very sad, but you would also know that because of that storm and that loss, your life's journey would take you somewhere you never would have gone before, and this somewhere would be the most amazing place you've ever been. What if you knew that you would meet the most important person in your life because you lost the person you loved the most? What if you saw the future and you knew that a series of misfortunes would have to come your way before the most amazing blessing would come? Would you still complain? Would you doubt that life would ever get any better? Would you go to bed worrying and fearful, or would you go to bed in peace, trusting his will and his rule?

The person who knows the future for the believer and knows that it is good never has anything to fear. Because they are certain of how everything works out, they can sit back and relax when others are panicked and grief stricken. This might sound impossible. You might be thinking, "You can never know the future, so what a pointless exercise!" but that's not exactly true. You can't know the future, that part is true, but you

can know that the future, whatever it might be, will be good because you know that the one whose hands you have put your future in is good.

Sometimes it's easier to see this in the lives of other people than in your own life, so let's just see how this played out in the life of someone who's long dead. Joseph was the youngest of twelve boys. (You can read the full story of Joseph in Genesis chapters 37 and 39–50. It's long but well worth the read.) He was his daddy's favorite, and because of that his brothers hated him. Joseph had dreams about the future. In the Old Testament times God often spoke to his people in dreams, so Joseph knew, if only in part, the future that awaited him, and he knew that it was good. But when he told this future to his brothers, they got very angry. They didn't like the idea that they would bow down to their little brother, so they hated him and wanted him dead. So began Joseph's really bad day. And that bad day turned into one bad day after another. He went from the pit they threw him in to leave him for dead to becoming an Egyptian slave boy to being sent to prison for a crime he didn't commit.

When life gets this ugly, it can be easy to doubt. It's easy to say things like "This isn't fair" and "What did I do to deserve this?" and "Where is God when bad things happen to me? Doesn't he love me enough to help?" These are the statements and questions that run through the mind set on things of this world. But those with a mind set on God never have to say these things, because they are certain of who holds the future and that he has their back. They might not know exactly what will happen next, but they know who wins the battle of life, and they know that God can be trusted with their future.

The Bible repeatedly makes it clear that God is good and that he is all-powerful. And a good and all-powerful God can be trusted. When he says to you, "I will work all things together for the good of those who love me" (see Rom. 8:28), he means it. When you fear, doubt, or worry, you call him a liar. You're saying, "The idea of God is great, but practically speaking, it's worthless to me. I need life to be good in order for me to believe that God cares." But remember Joseph? His life is a witness to the power of a bad day and messed-up life. Look at what happened in his life due in great part to his belief in the God of his future as well as his present.

The Bible tells us that when Joseph was bought as a slave by Potiphar, the captain of Pharaoh's guard, "The LORD was with Joseph, and he became a successful

man" in the house of Potiphar (Gen. 39:2 ESV). How can a slave ever be considered successful? How can such a terrible thing ever be good? With God all is possible. And for Joseph this bad thing in his life didn't destroy him but led to his success. Why? Because the Lord was with him.

Now, in order for the Lord to be with you, you have to believe, not doubt. James 1:6–7 says this about doubt and the presence of God: "the one who doubts is like a wave of the sea that is driven and tossed by the wind. For that person must not suppose that he will receive anything from the Lord" (ESV). **DOUBT IS A MIND DIVIDED BETWEEN TRUTH AND LIE.** It divides your allegiance and your faith and makes you unstable in everything you do. But a mind that is set on God, certain that he works out everything for good, has nothing to fear. God's character assures a carefree life. It's not necessarily an easy life, but it is a life without worry or fear. Certainty instead of doubt reigns in the life of those who set their minds on the truth about God rather than a lie.

Being sent to prison for something you didn't do, as Joseph was, is like being lied about, bullied, and isolated from everyone you know and love. There is nothing good about going to prison, from a worldly perspective. But when everything looked dark and the future that Joseph once dreamed of seemed more distant than ever, God was still at work in his life, making things come to pass and affecting situations, even bad situations, so that his plan would progress. Even when things seemed to be going backward instead of forward, Genesis 39:21 tells us that "the LORD was with Joseph and showed him steadfast love and gave him favor in the sight of the keeper of the prison" (ESV).

If Joseph hadn't been sold as a slave and thrown into prison, he never would have met the chief cupbearer to Pharaoh, and he never would have gotten to interpret his dream. But because he did do all those things, two years later Pharaoh heard about Joseph's gift of interpreting dreams and called Joseph out of prison to interpret his dream. This got Joseph, just a young Hebrew teenager, into the courts of Pharaoh, the ruler of Egypt. Soon he was given a position of leadership second only to Pharaoh himself. Everything in Joseph's life, from the age of seventeen, led him to this one crucial and magnificent moment. In this position Joseph was able to speak God's words to Pharaoh and ultimately save a generation of not only Egyptians but also fellow Hebrews. Under Joseph's leadership, the Egyptians prepared well for the

day of famine, and his family, including the eleven brothers who sold him as a slave those many years ago, was saved.

Did Joseph, after all those years and all that pain, resent his brothers for tearing him out of his family? No. Did he want to get revenge on them? No. Did he blame them for the evil they had done? Nope. Look what he said to them when they were sure he'd want to pay them back for what they had done: "As for you, you meant evil against me, but God meant it for good, to bring it about that many people should be kept alive, as they are today" (Gen. 50:20 ESV). Did you get that? When people mean things for evil, that doesn't translate to God also intending it for evil; instead he, being all good, means it all for your good. So when bad things happen to good people, we have to believe that the future requires the bad in order to bring about the good. When you are dealing with a broken and sinful race such as we humans are, bad stuff is bound to come to pass, but God, being perfect, still uses fallen humans to bring about his plans. He doesn't let the lives of his children amount to nothing. He doesn't let danger, trials, or terror divert his plans or weaken his hold on the lives of those who love him (see Prov. 21:1; Isa. 46:9–10).

A lot of the world looks at the death of Christ on that cross as a major failure—sheer pain and torture with nothing to be gained. The people who looked on mocked him and doubted him (see John 19:2–3; Luke 23:35, 39). They saw the blood, the water, and the tears, and they saw a failure. They saw the ultimately bad end to a really bad day. But this evil that they witnessed was required for our salvation. The bad produced the most important good in the life of mankind. The suffering of Christ led to our salvation. His pain became our strength and our freedom. And just as God used Christ's suffering for the ultimate good, so he uses your suffering for your good. Painful, terrible trials do not destroy a child of God; they instruct and move the child of God closer to the God they love (see Ps. 119:71; John 12:24; Phil. 1:29; Heb. 5:8).

The Brave know the truth, and the truth is that God works everything in the life of the believer for good. **NOTHING HAPPENS THAT IS OUTSIDE OF HIS CONTROL, AND NOTHING THAT HAPPENS IS A WASTE OR IS DESTRUCTIVE TO THE LIFE OF THE ONE WHO LOVES HIM.** The Brave show courage in the face of fearful and difficult situations because of their undying belief that God works all things together for the good of those who love him and have been called according to his purpose (see Rom. 8:28).

AS FOR YOU, YOU MEANT
EVIL AGAINST ME...

BUT GOD MEANT IT FOR GOOD, TO BRING IT ABOUT THAT MANY PEOPLE SHOULD BE KEPT ALIVE, AS THEY ARE TODAY.

GENESIS 50:20 ESV

THE BRAVE KNOW THE IDOLS IN THEIR LIVES

The world is full of idols—people, things, products, and ideas that are considered a great success and worshiped by many. Idols like singers, actors, shoe companies, tech companies, and sports teams all fight for the affections of your heart. Idolatry isn't just a thing of the past, for the ancient and uneducated man or woman, but is real and present in your life and the lives of those around you. The concept of idolatry is a big one, and more than we can cover in this section, but it's one that is essential for the Brave to understand, because your idols can steal your bravery right out from under you.

Idols aren't just statues and they aren't just famous people, but they can be anything you require in your life for happiness and hope. Idolatry is defined as an immoderate attachment or devotion to something other than God. **ANYTHING OTHER THAN GOD THAT YOU LOOK TO FOR ANYTHING GOD INTENDS TO GIVE YOU IS AN IDOL, A RIVAL TO GOD** (see Deut. 5:7; Matt. 6:24; Rom. 6:16). As such, it will slowly tear you away from the true source of your strength, wisdom, and hope.

The problem with idols is that they are breakable. They can be stolen, lost, killed, or damaged. Unlike

God, they are not eternal and not holy. They are not able to give you what they promise, and they'll almost always end up disappointing you. **BECAUSE IDOLS ARE SO WEAK AND IMPERFECT, THE FEAR OF LOSING THEM IS CONSTANT AND CONSUMING.** Because you set your heart on them so, because you love them and want them in your life, you continuously have to fret and stress over keeping them. **AN IDOL PUTS A LOT OF REQUIREMENTS ON ITS FOLLOWERS.** For example, the idol of comfort requires that everything be comfortable in order for the follower to be happy. When the worshiper of comfort isn't comfortable, they complain, whine, and doubt. They can't be happy or content. They can't go on, they can't survive, they can't do without the thing they need to bring them comfort. So the worshiper of comfort fears things like going somewhere where they will be uncomfortable or doing something that won't feel good. They panic, stress, and fear the unknown because of the fear of being uncomfortable and not serving the idol of comfort. Beyond being the terrible sin of idolatry, this also can quickly become the sin of disobedience when comfort speaks more loudly than the voice of God that says "go." When God wants you to do something or go somewhere and you won't because you fear the

discomfort involved, the idol of comfort has become king of your life.

But the Brave know the idols in their lives and choose to destroy them. When one pops up in their life, they smash it, like a spiritual game of Whack-a-Mole. When the idol of comfort, lust, or fear screams to be fed, the Brave resist it and instead turn to the God of love for satisfaction and relief. They won't split their love between God and stuff. They won't turn their back on God to focus solely on his creation. And they won't let themselves become consumed with anything other than God himself.

Idols need to be smashed in order for you to grow in your faith, but idols don't often take to being rejected. When you know your idols and refuse to follow, worship, or obey them, it might go badly for you at first, but the lives of God's people in Scripture who had to face these things can be of some encouragement. For example, look at the bravery that Daniel showed when the edict came down that no one could pray to anyone but the king for thirty days, and anyone who disobeyed would be thrown into the lions' den (see Dan. 6). Daniel didn't flinch. He went home, opened up the windows, and knelt down to pray to God. He didn't listen to the idol of his own comfort and safety.

He was bent on serving the living God no matter what threatened him if he did.

What gave Daniel the courage to obey God even when the world promised pain if he did? His knowledge of who God was and who was not a god but just part of creation. The bravery that it took to not only continue to pray to God but also walk into the lions' den without argument or terror was born in his knowledge of the holy and how God would protect Daniel's soul, if not his flesh, from any terror or destruction that man or beast could bring. **WHEN GOD IS TRUSTED, THE SOUL IS SAFE, AND THE BRAVE PROVE TO THE WORLD WHO GOD IS.** Look at how the king described God after seeing how he had saved Daniel from the lions: "He is the living God, enduring forever; his kingdom shall never be destroyed, and his dominion shall be to the end. He delivers and rescues; he works signs and wonders in heaven and on earth, he who has saved Daniel from the power of the lions" (Dan. 6:26–27 ESV). The brave in Daniel was fed by his unstoppable belief and faith in the goodness and protection of God, and it resulted in the world seeing God at work in the life of one who would only believe and would not doubt, no matter how much the world and all he saw around him would tell him to do otherwise.

Like Joseph, Daniel had more than a few bad days, as we've already seen. His country was invaded and his home destroyed. He was carried away as a teenager, made to become a slave in a foreign land. His life was anything but normal, but he never stopped believing. He never doubted or turned or said "Why me?" He was convinced that no matter what, only God deserves our worship, and because of that he refused to serve idols.

While you'll probably never be a slave to a foreign king or face the capital punishment of being eaten by lions, you'll still have to fight your own battles against idols to keep your focus on God so you can stay brave. When the battle rages, don't be surprised, and know you are not alone. We all must fight the fight against our idols, knowing that to give in and to serve the stuff that struggles for control of our lives is to lose not only the battle but also the war.

THE BRAVE KNOW WEAKNESS IS STRENGTH

The Brave aren't any more special than the fearful. They aren't superhuman or superheroes; they are just ordinary people who have learned something that the rest of the world hasn't learned. They have learned that things aren't always as they appear, that up isn't always up and down isn't always down, but what looks like a bad thing might actually be the best thing that could happen, and what seems like an impossible thing to survive might actually be a requirement for survival. The Brave look at life differently than the average person. They don't see what the world sees, but they see beyond. They see the strength of God in their weakness and his power in their trials. The Brave understand that the battle isn't theirs and that the requirement for success is faith, not brute strength.

The Brave sometimes get confused with the stupid, because what they do seems impossible and what they risk, crazy. But the Brave see the world not through the eyes of the flesh but the eyes of the spirit. They see what can only be seen by faith, so they see things as they really are and not as they pretend to be. This is why the Brave see weakness as strength. It seems like a ridiculous statement, calling something what it isn't, but nothing could be more true. In the life of faith, the way up is oftentimes the way down, and the power that you need to be brave is the weakness that you show when you fall down to your knees and lower yourself so that God might be lifted up. Admitting you

are powerless, confessing your weakness, and trusting in his strength is another key to putting the brave in your life.

Take a look at the life of Paul. Paul was well aware of his weaknesses. He referred to life as a delicate and weak jar of clay. Why? Follow his line of reasoning in 2 Corinthians 4:7–11 (ESV):

> But we have this treasure in jars of clay, to show that the surpassing power belongs to God and not to us. We are afflicted in every way, but not crushed; perplexed, but not driven to despair; persecuted, but not forsaken; struck down, but not destroyed; always carrying in the body the death of Jesus, so that the life of Jesus may also be manifested in our bodies. For we who live are always being given over to death for Jesus' sake, so that the life of Jesus also may be manifested in our mortal flesh.

Did you get that? We are weak so that everyone can see that the surpassing power belongs to God and not to us! That's good news. Whose power is better, yours or his? Why wouldn't you want to claim his over yours when his is so much more awesome?

Your weakness is meant to be not the end of you but the beginning of him. If you can agree with this, then you can live like Paul did when everything threatened to destroy him. Even though life was hard, even treacherous, this is what Paul said in 2 Corinthians 12:8–10 (ESV) about his suffering:

> Three times I pleaded with the Lord about this, that it should leave me. But he said to me, "My grace is sufficient for you, for my power is made perfect in weakness." Therefore I will boast all the more gladly of my weaknesses, so that the power of Christ may rest upon me. For the sake of Christ, then, I am content with weaknesses, insults, hardships, persecutions, and calamities. For when I am weak, then I am strong.

When you are content with whatever comes your way, fearing nothing, then the brave and you are one. You have found the brave, my friend, and it is good. Then you will be able to say with the psalmist, "The Lord is my light and my salvation. Who is there to fear? The Lord is my life's fortress. Who is there to be afraid of?" (Ps. 27:1). The bravery that withstands all is available to all who put their faith in the Lord as their light and their salvation, knowing that their weakness only speaks to his strength.

BE FIRM IN THE FAITH
AND RESIST [THE DEVIL],
KNOWING THAT OTHER
BELIEVERS THROUGHOUT
THE WORLD ARE GOING
THROUGH THE SAME KIND
OF SUFFERING.

GOD, WHO SHOWS YOU HIS KINDNESS AND WHO HAS CALLED YOU THROUGH CHRIST JESUS TO HIS ETERNAL GLORY, WILL RESTORE YOU, STRENGTHEN YOU, MAKE YOU STRONG, AND SUPPORT YOU AS YOU SUFFER FOR A LITTLE WHILE. POWER BELONGS TO HIM FOREVER. AMEN.

1 PETER 5:9-11

The Brave love the truth, and in order to love the truth, they must pursue it, go after it, seek it. It's easy to be scared. It's easy to panic, to fear, and to worry, because you can make it up as you go. There is no truth behind these things, so the foundation for all panic, fear, and worry is whatever will help you to doubt the goodness and the omnipotence of God. But the truth will set you free from your doubt and your fear and make you a part of the Brave. The truth must be an essential part of your life; without it the lies of the enemy will creep in and control you. You will not be your own; you will be a victim of your lies. In order to find the brave in your life, you must find the places where you've believed a lie and replace that lie with the truth. If you've believed that God wasn't good enough or strong enough to make your suffering into glory, then replace that lie with the truth: "Be happy as you share Christ's sufferings. Then you will also be full of joy when he appears again in his glory" (1 Pet. 4:13).

CHAPTER

4

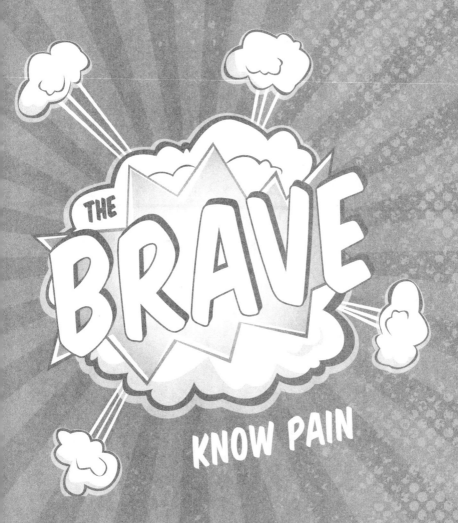

THE BRAVE

KNOW PAIN

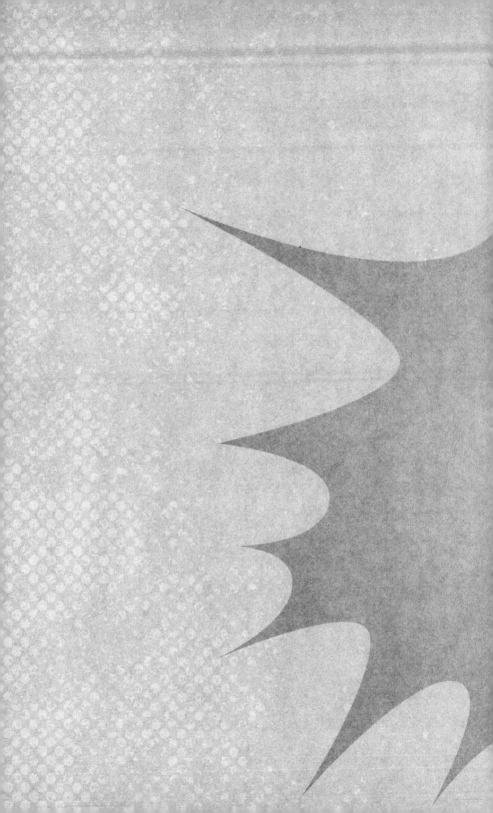

AT THE ROOT OF ALL FEAR IS THE IDEA THAT PAIN IS ON ITS WAY AND THAT PAIN IS BAD AND TO BE AVOIDED AT ALL COSTS. The fearful run in the opposite direction of pain, while the Brave stand and face it, even run toward it when necessary, knowing that the gain they will find on the other side will make all of the pain worthwhile. Your thoughts on pain, then, are the barometer of your emotional life and the presence or lack of the brave stuff in your life.

In this world you will have pain. You will be rejected, hurt, sick, and even dying. Pain is a part of life, and what you think about pain is a very important part of who you are. Knowing the truth about pain sets the Brave free because the truth makes sense of injury, loss, and agony. In a world where pain has no purpose other than to slowly suck the life out of a person, pain is an unwelcome and feared thing. But in the life of the Brave, pain serves a great purpose.

The Brave know pain, and therefore they know gain. The gain that they get from the pain in their life isn't masochistic but spiritual. **PAIN SERVES A PURPOSE, AND THAT PURPOSE ISN'T TO DESTROY YOU BUT TO MAKE YOU STRONGER.** The fearful avoid pain and dread its appearance because they haven't fully understood its value. Now, before you scream, "Value? There's no value to being in pain!" just give pain a chance and listen to what we have to say before you give up on the idea of finding bravery in your pain.

TO KNOW THE PAIN IN YOUR LIFE AND TO FIND GAIN IN IT IS TO KNOW THE GOD IN YOUR LIFE AND TO FIND HIM GOOD. Nothing happens, not even pain, unless God in his great goodness allows it for his perfect purposes. The Israelites suffered a lot in the days of Jeremiah, but God had this to say about their pain: "As I brought all these disasters on these people, so I will bring on them all these blessings that I have promised them" (Jer. 32:42). God doesn't disappear when hard times come; he isn't absent and out of touch but is very much a part of every aspect of your life. As a believer you have to know that **GOD DOESN'T SAVE YOU FROM PAIN BUT IN PAIN.** That means that pain serves a great purpose, and this is where the Brave find their power: they see purpose in their pain rather than uselessness and nonsense. They see the amazing power that pain can have in their lives, and they believe the words they read in Philippians 1:29: "God has given you the privilege not only to believe in Christ but also to suffer for him."

Pain, suffering, and struggles are all part of life for every human being on earth, but for the Brave they are gain because they are all under the control of their perfect, trustworthy, and faithful Father. He not only works everything together for their good but also promises a great reward for those who suffer and yet keep the faith all the while (see Matt. 5:11–12; Rom. 5:3–4; 8:17; 2 Cor. 4:17–18; Heb. 12:10).

For the Brave, pain serves a far greater purpose than destruction and diversion. **PAIN SERVES THE PURPOSE OF FORCING THEM TO RELY COMPLETELY ON GOD.** In 2 Corinthians 1:8–9 Paul says it like this:

> Brothers and sisters, we don't want you to be ignorant about the suffering we experienced in the province of Asia. It was so extreme that it was beyond our ability to endure. We even wondered if we could go on living. In fact, we still feel as if we're under a death sentence. But we suffered so that we would stop trusting ourselves and learn to trust God, who brings the dead back to life.

Paul's pain served an amazing purpose: it taught him to stop trusting himself and to start trusting God. But this is only true because Paul knew the source of everything in his life, and that made him a part of the Brave. Charles Spurgeon, the famous pastor, was intimately aware of the gain of pain. He suffered from severe gout and bouts with depression, and he could not bear to think of it as being from anyone but God himself. He said, "It would be a very sharp and trying experience to me to think that I have an affliction which God never sent me, that the bitter cup was never filled by his hand, that my trials were never measured out by him, nor sent to me by his arrangement of their weight and quantity."[3] The Brave know who has their life in his hands, and because of that they can know pain and know gain.

Pain is a great teacher in the life of the Brave. It's worth reading one more thing that came out of the painful life of Spurgeon, just to show you how faith receives the trial of pain. Take a look at his wishes for others: "I dare say the greatest earthly blessing that God can give to any of us is health, with the exception of sickness. . . . If some men that I know of could only be favored with a month of rheumatism, it would, by God's grace, mellow them marvelously."[4] The Bible agrees with this idea of mellowing, or maturing, a person through pain when it talks about faithfully persevering through pain so that you can become "mature and complete, not lacking anything" (James 1:4 NIV). So pain is the great maturer. The Brave, who live through great pain successfully without allowing it to become the end of them or to tear them away from their faith, mature at a far quicker rate than others their age. From the pain comes all kinds of wisdom, grace, compassion, and faith for those who are willing to accept the perseverance that it requires. You can cling to and remember this purpose of pain whenever pain threatens to be your destruction. Always remember that it cannot destroy you, but it can bring you growth and maturity beyond your years.

You might not trust God enough just yet to accept the pain in your life, but the pain will get you there, because the pain is what produces endurance. No pain, no gain. Know pain, know gain. You can be happy when you run into problems and trials, because those trials develop your endurance. And endurance builds your strength of character, and your strength of character builds up your confidence in your salvation, not just for heaven, but from the sins of this world as well. And guess what? This hope doesn't disappoint,

because God loves you so much that he has given you the Holy Spirit to fill your heart with his very own love (see Rom. 5:3–5). Bang! Welcome to the land of the free and the home of the Brave. God's Word confirms it: you have all you need inside of you to endure, and endure well, anything that comes your way. The Holy Spirit is on your side. He isn't watching from a distance but lives inside of you, actively moving in your life. And because of that nothing—not trouble, distress, persecution, hunger, nakedness, danger, or violent death—can separate you from his love (see Rom. 8:35–39). This is the way the Brave live—not by their own strength but by his. And it's the way you can live too.

This might seem like anything but the truth when you are in the throes of pain, but the Bible promises that you can "consider those who endure to be blessed" (James 5:11). Blessings await endurance. One of those blessings is that pain teaches you compassion. Second Corinthians 1:4 says that when you suffer and let God comfort you, showing you his compassion, it has an amazing side effect: that "whenever other people suffer, we are able to comfort them by using the same comfort we have received from God." Pain teaches your soul compassion so that you aren't out just for yourself, but you become aware of the pain around you and also know how to respond to it with help and comfort, just like you have been comforted. So pain serves the purpose of making you able to help and to comfort others.

PAIN IS NOT GOD'S WEAPON USED TO DESTROY YOU BUT HIS TOOL USED TO TEACH AND GROW YOU. He doesn't inflict pain to torture you but allows it to mature you. Sometimes pain comes as a result of sin, in the form of discipline, but sometimes pain has nothing at all to do with sin. In fact, the pain that Jesus endured is evidence of that. He had no sin in him at all, and yet he endured all the pain in the world in one day. But this pain served a great purpose—not only the salvation of mankind but also his own obedience. Hebrews 5:8 teaches us another purpose of pain: "Although Jesus was the Son of God, he learned to be obedient through his sufferings." Your pain can serve the purpose of teaching you obedience as well, if you are willing to trust him with your pain. Can you be willing, when the aches come, when the heart breaks, and when the prognosis isn't good, to accept the comfort of God and to trust that he has a great purpose for the pain in your life? If you are, then you have become one of the Brave.

THE BRAVE DON'T WORRY ABOUT FUTURE PAIN

> I'm giving you my peace. I don't give you the kind
> of peace that the world gives. So don't be troubled
> or cowardly. (John 14:27)

While fear has to do with the arrival of pain, worry ponders the fear of future pain. This pain may or may not ever come, but worry promises that if we think about it long enough, we might overcome it. Worry tells us that the more we concentrate on a problem, the more the concentrated energy of our thoughts will protect us from what we fear and maybe even keep it from happening. Worry is your body on alert, guarding itself, pacing the wall, keeping an eye out for enemies, trigger finger ready. But the trouble is that it has no bullets, nothing to hurl at intruders to stun them or disable them. So they just keep on coming. Worry is powerless to do what its express purpose is: to protect you.

As we've mentioned, when Hayley was younger, she was afraid of flying. She was on the verge of a panic attack every time she got onto a plane. She worried so much about crashing that she *had* to have a window seat so she could monitor things outside the plane. The idea of not being able to see outside was like the idea of driving a car with a blindfold on. Her worry needed comfort, and the comfort it got was from believing that it was safer for her to look out the window than to sit on the aisle, as if the pilot needed her eyes in order to keep the plane up in the air. Closing the shade and choosing not to look out the window was not an option to her worried mind. She was scared to death, and worrying was the only way she could feel any control over the situation. Worry believes it is active and in control, while faith is inactive and not in control.

But the activity of worry is deceiving. It pretends to be really busy, watching for rogue planes coming into its airspace, keeping an eye out for storm clouds and lightning bolts. Worry has a big job, or so it says. "I've got my hands full just thinking about everything that could go wrong," says worry. Worry promises comfort to the fearful, hope to the helpless, and safety to the anxious.

Worry is all about protecting you from whatever it is you dread the most. It feeds on your anxiety that whatever you fear would be terrible, horrible, and un- bearable. Worry works as hard as it can to protect you from pain. Pain, or the fear of it, is the fuel of all worry. At the root of everything that consumes you is this idea that if a certain thing happens you will suffer, and

in your mind, pain is a bad, bad thing. So you worry about friends, you worry about disaster, you worry about pain. You worry that you will lose something, that you will have to do something, or that you will find out something. Worry is an early protection system for your heart, and it does its best to guard against any kind of pain or suffering that might be coming.

But while worry is promising to protect you, it's silently destroying you. Worry makes you sick to your stomach with uneasiness. It makes it hard to fall asleep, which makes you tired and grumpy. It makes you anxious and panicked. It gives you headaches and sore muscles. It makes you nauseated and nervous. Thus it ends up giving you an early down payment on the thing that you are worried about—pain—in the form of self-inflicted pain. Worry trades imagined pain for real pain and future stress for current stress, and it keeps you from living a life that is effective and strong.

Oddly enough, **WHAT THE WORRIER IS FEARING MIGHT BE THE VERY THING THAT GOD IS ALLOWING.** Remember that if it happens to you, then God allowed it to happen, such as the destruction Satan let loose on Job, but only after getting God's permission (see Job 1). In Lamentations 3:37–38 this truth is crystallized when it says, "Who was it who spoke and it came into being?

It was the Lord who gave the order. Both good and bad come from the mouth of the Most High God." That means that **NOTHING IS OUT OF GOD'S CONTROL, NOT EVEN THE PAIN YOU ARE SUFFERING OR MIGHT SUFFER TOMORROW.** So if God is going to allow some pain to come into your life, why would you argue with him and tell him that you are afraid of his choices for your life, as if your choices would be better ones? It might sound impossible right now to not fear future pain, but ask yourself this: "Would I rather have God's will for my life, no matter how painful, or my own, no matter how ungodly?" You're choosing the latter when you worry. Worry says, "God, your choices for my life might be too dangerous, too ugly, and too bad for me, and my choices, my dreams, and my hopes are perfect, and without them I cannot go on." Is that really what you think—that you are wiser and a better judge of what's best for you than your perfect heavenly Father? That's what worry says.

THIS IDEA OF BELIEVING THE BEST INSTEAD OF WOR-RYING ABOUT THE HARD STUFF HAS ITS FOUNDATION IN FAITH, but researchers at Harvard and Yale universities recently found the same to be true when they conducted a study. It is a little-known fact that stress can actually *enhance* the human brain and body when it

is looked at properly, and the researchers proved this point when they showed two groups of stressed people two different videos. The first group saw a three-minute video on the effects of stress and worry on the body. This group got stressed-out by the video. The second group watched a video that talked about how stress can actually improve the ability of your brain to function. They were taught that it can improve your memory and intelligence, increase your productivity, and even speed up your recovery from things like knee surgery. This group, unlike the first, didn't stress out, because they were comforted by the knowledge of the benefits of their stress. They learned that stress can make you more mentally tough and give you deeper relationships, a heightened awareness, a new perspective on life, a sense of mastery over something, an appreciation for life, and a heightened sense of meaning. It can even strengthen your priorities. Because they began to see the benefits found in a degree of stress, they were more relaxed than the first group.[5]

Like the group that got knowledge rather than more stress over stress, the Brave are set free from the domination of worry because they are so certain of God's goodness that they can let go of their death grip on their future and their panic over the present. They can

say, "Whatever he wills is the best for me." They can
stop all worry in their lives because of the certainty that
God is in control and that no matter how bad things
look, he can be trusted.

THE BRAVE ARE CONFIDENT

The Brave know that the pain that might or might not
come into their lives isn't something to fear but a chance
to trust, so they are set free from worry. But what about
those times when you say, "Sure, I can trust God—I
just can't trust myself. I'm going to mess things up, not
him"? This kind of self-doubt or insecurity can be a
major problem, especially in relationships with other
human beings. Out of this come feelings of shyness,
self-loathing, insecurity, and low self-esteem. Those
feelings don't belong in the life of faith, because they
are all the result of focusing on the wrong thing. The
subject of all these bad feelings isn't God but self. It's
no wonder you have doubt in yourself, because you
aren't perfect, you are human, you are broken, and
you don't know everything. Of course, making you
the focus of life is going to disappoint!

But the Brave aren't focused inward. They don't live
to serve the good of themselves. If they did, they would

have no reason to rise above the sensation of pain to serve one greater than themselves, because none would be greater. Low self-esteem, self-loathing, and insecurity might look like symptoms of a low view of who you are, but the truth is, they are actually a high and prideful view of who you are. Sounds impossible, but it's true: those feelings of self-defeat, worthlessness, and grief over a miserable life have at their root the idea that you deserve better and that you are such a special case that no one else could possibly be as bad off as you. You are in fact the "worst" person in the world, which in a weird twist of self-obsession means you are in one way more incredible than others because you have achieved more in the area of misery, weakness, or grief than anyone before or since you. **PRIDE FOCUSES ON SELF AND MAKES SELF THE CENTER OF THE UNIVERSE.** When that's the case, you believe every bad thing that happens, happens to you, every evil person in the world is sent to destroy you, every bad day was made just for you, and on and on. **THIS INWARD-FOCUSED WAY OF THINKING MAKES YOUR LIFE THE STAR AND PUTS CHRIST IN THE BACKSEAT.**

THE BRAVE SEE A DIFFERENT STORY: THEY SEE THEIR LIVES AS UNWORTHY OF THE SUFFERING OF CHRIST. Charles Spurgeon, who we mentioned earlier, said,

"Your pains are sharp, yet 'his strokes are fewer than your crimes, and lighter than your guilt.' From the pains of hell Christ has delivered you. Why should a living man complain? As long as you are out of hell, gratitude may mingle with your groans."[6] The Brave see that they don't deserve to have even a day of happiness because of the depth of their sinfulness, so they are invigorated and inspired by the fact that God was so gracious to them that he sent his one and only Son to take on their sin so that they might live forever, even though they have time and again turned their backs on God. The Brave know that there is no one who is righteous, not even one (see Rom. 3:10), so they aren't surprised by their weakness or their sinfulness. They don't condemn what God has forgiven. Sure, they confess their sin, but they also accept the immediate forgiveness that God offers to all who confess (see 1 John 1:9). They don't hold on to their sin as if God isn't big enough to take it away or to forgive and forget it, removing it as far as the east is from the west (see Ps. 103:12).

The Brave have confidence not in themselves but in God. You might say that they too lack self-esteem but have replaced it with God-esteem. Any time you find all your value and goodness in who you are, you will be disappointed sooner or later, because you will

fail. But when you find your value in who he is, you will never be disappointed. The Brave are confident because of who God is. They aren't consumed with the fear of pleasing other people because that isn't their goal; pleasing God is all they want to do. So when God commands them to love others (see John 13:34–35), to show hospitality (1 Pet. 4:9), and to show compassion and mercy (see Zech. 7:9), they don't have the luxury of labeling themselves as too shy or introverted, because they have decided this life is not about them and their failures but about him and his victory.

If you are shy by nature, it doesn't have to be a life sentence. Your weaknesses can be turned into strengths when you don't hold on to them for dear life but let them be transformed by the renewing power of his grace (2 Cor. 5:17). Faith changes things. It makes the scared, brave and the shy, outgoing. It makes the old way of the flesh outdated and unacceptable and makes the new way of the Spirit the only way to go.

THE BRAVE HAVE VICTORY OVER THE PAIN INFLICTED BY THE THOUGHTS AND ACTIONS OF OTHER PEOPLE BECAUSE THEY NO LONGER LIVE FOR THEMSELVES. They are soldiers in the army of God, so they don't let themselves get involved in civilian affairs anymore but take their orders from their commander and trust that the war is under his control (see 2 Tim. 2:4). All the Brave have to do is follow commands, not protect themselves or resist the commander's call to "Charge!" The Brave are never insecure, because all their security is found in the rock of their salvation, the one who never changes and who can always be trusted (see Num. 23:19; Jer. 17:7). What they know of pain because of this is that "suffering creates endurance, endurance creates character, and character creates confidence" (Rom. 5:3–4). *OUT OF THE ENDURING PAIN THEY GAIN THE CONFIDENCE THAT OTHERS CAN NEVER FIND.* This confidence might not come easy, but it is strong and enduring, and once you have it, you will never fear others again.

THE BRAVE ACCEPT FAILURE

If you're following us so far, you probably can also believe that the Brave accept failure. *FAILURE IS SUB-JECTIVE. ONE MAN'S FAILURE MIGHT JUST BE ANOTHER MAN'S VICTORY.* It's how you look at it that affects what impact it makes on your life. The Brave look at failure in light of who God is, not who they are. Failure, if it has the fingerprints of God on it, is just turning you away from the wrong direction and toward the right

one. And the Brave are certain that God's fingerprints are on *all* parts of their lives when they are going after and trusting in his perfect will. **THE BRAVE CATEGORIZE FAILURE INTO TWO CAMPS. ONE KIND OF FAILURE COMES FROM SINNING.** When you don't do what God commands you to do, failure is bound to follow. When you refuse to submit to authority, failure comes in the form of discipline, sometimes called punishment, from those in authority over you. Failure comes when you don't do what God commands because what God commands is meant for your good. That means that the result of not obeying is going to be something bad. So **FAILURE SERVES TO TEACH YOU NOT TO DO SOMETHING THAT ISN'T GOOD FOR YOU. THIS KIND OF FAILURE IS CALLED DISCIPLINE** (see Lam. 3:39; Heb. 12:6).

While discipline can be uncomfortable and no fun to live through, it is meant for your good. So the Brave say "thank you" when discipline shapes and corrects them, and they don't let the pain of discipline or the sting of failure get the better of them.

The Brave don't confuse this discipline in the form of failure with God's will for their lives. For example, the Brave don't sin and then blame their failure in life on him. An example of this would be a person who knew that God forbids premarital sex having it anyway,

getting a sexually transmitted disease, and then saying, "It must be God's will that I'm sick now." No, it is
never God's will for his people to sin, and that's why he
disciplines them. So the result of sin is God's discipline,
not God's perfect will. Making you more like Christ
for God's glory is his will. Discipline is different than
God's judgment. Take for example the sin of divorce.[7]
It is never okay to say, "Well, God sure blessed my
divorce." God doesn't bless sin. But God does allow
failure to become a blessing when you learn from it,
take the consequences as good discipline, and agree
that God's way is perfect and your failure to follow his
will is what led to your failure in this area of life.

But what about the second kind of failure—when
you are looking to please God and that ends in failure?
How can you look at that failure in a good light? Think
about it like this: failure is a lot like God shutting a door
that it wouldn't be best for you to go through. **FAILURE
ISN'T ALWAYS THE RESULT OF SIN BUT CAN BE PART
OF GOD'S PERFECT WILL.** Think about the life of Moses.
God told him to go back to Egypt and tell the Pharaoh
to set his people free. God ordered Moses to do this,
but when Moses did what he was told, he failed. Not
just once, but nine times. That was through no fault of
his own but because God hardened Pharaoh's heart

(Exod. 14:8), which means it was all a part of God's plan. So when you obey God, you can't get all dramatic over how you must not have heard him right because you failed. Maybe, just maybe, you did hear him and failure was what he required in that moment.

THE ONLY HARD AND FAST RULE ABOUT FAILURE IS THAT YOU CAN NEVER LET FAILURE DEFEAT YOU. The Brave have courage in the face of failure, because they don't see failure as an attack from the enemy or as a failure of God's plan or God's law, but they see it as evidence of God's hand on their life, giving it what he will give it and taking from it what he will take. Failure isn't the end for the Brave but is the next step on the road to faith. The Brave let failure do its work, driving them to repentance and to an undying trust in the sovereignty of God.

THE BRAVE UNDERSTAND TRIALS

For the Brave, everything can be used for good. The Brave don't let anything in their lives go to waste—not their pain or their failure and most definitely not their trials. Trial is the stuff that faith is made of. In the beginning of the book of James, as we peeked at earlier, these famous words were penned:

> Consider it pure joy, my brothers and sisters, when-
> ever you face trials of many kinds, because you know
> that the testing of your faith produces perseverance.
> Let perseverance finish its work so that you may be
> mature and complete, not lacking anything. (James
> 1:2–4 NIV)

Not only are trials something that make your life better, but they are something that should be considered
pure joy. Huh? Sounds impossible! But for the Brave,
who are certain that everything serves God's purposes,
it is not. Joy can be a part of your trials too when you
see each trial as a tool of sanctification instead of destruction. Sanctification is the ongoing process that is
moving you toward holiness and away from the sin that
used to be yours. Sanctification is purifying, strength-
ening, and invigorating. And while it often involves
some pain, it's a good kind of pain, the kind of pain
that you feel when you lift weights. Weight lifters get
the idea of know pain, know gain. The muscles have
to be torn in order for them to be rebuilt stronger than
they were before. This tearing can hurt and make you
sore for days, but it's easier to bear when you know
what the pain is doing to your body. When you think
about what the result will be once the muscles grow
back, you can be joyful in the midst of the pain. But

if you think the pain is the be-all and end-all and that you can't bear the pain, then your failure to see the end result will end up making your pain worse than it needs to be.

The Brave understand that in the life of faith, it's the same kind of thing. ***TRIALS AND PAIN ALL CAN BE USED FOR GOD WHEN YOUR LOVE FOR HIM OUTWEIGHS YOUR FEAR OF THE PAIN THAT YOU MIGHT HAVE TO LIVE THROUGH IN ORDER TO BE CHANGED MORE INTO THE IMAGE OF HIS SON.*** The Brave believe every word when they read that "The purpose of these troubles is to test your faith as fire tests how genuine gold is. Your faith is more precious than gold, and by passing the test, it gives praise, glory, and honor to God" (1 Pet. 1:7).

Your trials aren't meant to destroy you, so they don't have to be feared but can be faced with bravery and courage. ***FOR PEOPLE WHO BLAME THEIR TRIALS ON THE ENEMY OF GOD, SUFFERING PAIN CAN BE AN UGLY THING.*** No one wants to suffer at the hands of the devil, but to that we say, "Why would you give the devil so much power?" Satan isn't God, so he isn't all-powerful. He has to have God's permission to operate in this world (see Job 1). So the real person to think about when trials come your way is God himself. Knowing what you know to be true about his goodness and kindness, what can you conclude about your trials but that they are for your good? Giving God the power in your trials takes it away from the enemy. The Brave get this and don't let themselves serve the fear of God's enemy but instead fear God himself and his awesomeness and power.

The Brave understand trials and the pain they might promise, and they refuse to let them be used for evil. They take each trial as a gift from God and wait with confident anticipation for the ultimate deliverance that God will bring to the life of the faithful. Even if they will see relief only on the other side of eternity, in heaven itself, they will still stand confident in God's goodness and control of any and every situation, knowing that what awaits them when they die will be completely worth it all.

The Brave know gain in life because they know pain and they put it in its rightful place. Pain is unavoidable, and sometimes it's going to be uncontrollable as well. You are going to face times in your life when no habit will stop the ache and when no drug will take away the continual pain. You are going to have hard times in life, no doubt, but when you have an accurate view of what you live for, who you serve, and why you exist,

then no pain can derail you from your path. You have to remember that pain is meant not to destroy you but to put you back at the feet of the Father. Pain directs your steps and forces you to rely completely on him. If he wills it, then you have to know that it's the best for you right now.

Accept the hand of God on your life. Know the value of a healthy understanding of stress and pain, and don't let that value be lost on your worry, doubt, or fear, but use it all for good. Take God at his word and know pain in order to know gain.

THE BRAVE

CONQUER THEIR FEAR

YOU HAVE TWO CHOICES IN LIFE: EITHER YOU CAN CONQUER YOUR FEAR, OR YOUR FEAR CAN CONQUER YOU. There are no other options; you can't peacefully coexist with your fear, because fear won't allow it. Fear fights for control. It fights to establish its godship in your life. You can either give in to it or resist it. In the case of good fear, as in the fear of God, giving in to that fear is the best thing you can do. Then you have given God his rightful place, allowing him to call the shots in your life and to move you to action. But in the case of bad fear, which is most fear, giving in to it is giving it the place that God should have. For example, we have a friend who is afraid of flying, but unlike us, he doesn't have to fly for work. Well, maybe he's more afraid of crashing than flying, but either way, his fear is so strong that it rules his life. So when God called our friend to go to Africa to serve, he said no, because his fear trumped his God—or in this case, became his god.

Either your fear can conquer you, making you a slave to it, or you can conquer it. But conquering fear is an enormous proposition. For centuries humans have been controlled by their fear. They have missed opportunities, destroyed families, committed sins, and fought wars all at the foot of fear. Fear is a powerful force in this life, which is why an even more powerful force is required to overrule it. Your fight against fear will be a failure until you turn it over to the only one who can win it. If the brave in your life has been elusive, then have we got news for you: it won't be anymore, because now you know the secret to the brave in this life, and that is that it doesn't come from you. It isn't possible for you to fight such a powerful foe. You don't have the strength, but you do have someone you can rely on who does have the strength. He has given you his Spirit to live inside you not only to guide and counsel you but also to give you the power to live a life out from under the control of fear.

This is good news! This means that **JUST LIKE YOUR SALVATION, THE BRAVE THAT YOU LONG FOR ISN'T UP TO YOUR STRENGTH OR YOUR WILL BUT SIMPLY REQUIRES YOUR FAITH IN THE ONE WHO SAVES.** In the book of Galatians, Paul gets on the people of Galatia for trying to do life in their own strength. It's a really good kick in the pants for anyone who thinks that by pulling up your sleeves and digging in your feet, you can get the brave into your life. Take a read and see what we mean. Paul starts right off, "You stupid people of Galatia!" (3:1). Ouch, they must have really messed up to earn such harsh language. But look at what comes next:

> Who put you under an evil spell? Wasn't Christ Jesus' crucifixion clearly described to you? I want to learn only one thing from you. Did you receive the Spirit by your own efforts to live according to a set of standards or by believing what you heard? Are you that stupid? Did you begin in a spiritual way only to end up doing things in a human way? (Gal. 3:1–3)

Did you catch that? You (and us), like the "stupid" Galatians, were saved by the Spirit of God and by his Spirit only. It wasn't any amazing feat accomplished by you; all you had to do was believe. He did all the rest. So why have you been trying, through your own brute strength, to fight the fear in your life when the same way you were saved is the same way you will find your brave?

THE BRAVE LIVE BY FAITH

THE BRAVE AREN'T BRAVE BECAUSE OF WHO THEY ARE BUT BECAUSE OF WHO GOD IS. And the brave you want in your life isn't out of your reach as long as you are reaching for the Holy Spirit who lives inside of you. In Galatians 5:22 Paul goes on to talk about what the Spirit of God in you does for you when he lists the fruit of the Spirit. The fruit of the Spirit is the stuff that comes into your life because of God living in you. It's the stuff that his Spirit supplies to you, allows in you, and gifts you with. It is the evidence of the life of God in you, and it is all you need to conquer the fear, pain, and suffering that threaten your life. Whenever you need to find the courage to go on, to believe, to stand, to rest, to know—whenever you are faced with trials, with pain, with suffering—if you can respond to those times in peace and patience with a dash of self-control, then you have lived life as the bravest of the Brave. And that is exactly what you can get, not from your own hard work but from the Spirit inside of you.

Galatians 5 lists these nine qualities as the fruit of the Spirit: "love, joy, *peace*, *patience*, kindness, goodness, faithfulness, gentleness, and *self-control*" (vv. 22–23, emphasis added). Did you see that? Peace in moments of terror, doubt, worry, fear, or danger comes from the Spirit, not your own strength. Patience when things wear on you, threaten you, or tug at you comes from the Spirit, not from your own hard work. And self-control when you want to give up, give in, or do what you shouldn't do comes from the Spirit, not you! When you live by the Spirit, you have all you need to become one of the Brave.

THE BRAVE IN YOUR LIFE DOESN'T COME FROM YOU; IT COMES FROM GOD IN YOU. In the pursuit of brave, these words can be your guide: "Not by might, nor by power, but by my Spirit, says the LORD of hosts" (Zech. 4:6 ESV). It isn't through you that you overcome the hard parts of your life. Maybe you thought it was; maybe you've tried your hardest and still you've failed. Thank God! That means that his Word is true. *THE BRAVE AREN'T MADE BY PEOPLE BUT BY GOD.* So if you want to consistently respond to the hard parts of life with peace, patience, and self-control, stop looking to yourself and start letting God be all that he wants to be for you.

Hopefully you get the idea by now, but how exactly does this happen? How do you do nothing while God does everything? You do it by turning your life and your trials over to him. You do that by making yourself small

and him enormous. You do that by making life not all about you but all about him. You do that by living by faith and not by sight. The Brave know the source of their strength, so they call on that source over anything else, and they do that in four ways. Let's dig into those ways now.

THE BRAVE PRAY

In your life there are a lot of impossible things to be overcome: impossible assignments, impossible pain, impossible change. Impossible stuff is frightening and can make you throw your hands up in the air and give up. But in the words of E. M. Bounds, "Faith does the impossible because it brings God to undertake for us, and nothing is impossible with God."[8] The Brave are not brave because of what they do or who they are but because of who God is and what he does. Because of that, "impossible" holds little meaning to them.

On this earth there will always be immovable obstacles and forces that threaten to crush you. But the Brave have hope, because the Brave have access to the Creator of all through the discipline of prayer. Have you heard the expression "prayer moves mountains"? It comes from the words of Jesus in Mark 11:23, where he told his followers that if they believe, then they can pray for a mountain to "be uprooted and thrown into the sea," and it will be done for them. These are some powerful words, and they're words that most of us don't really believe, if we are honest with ourselves. But maybe that's because we don't really understand the concept. A more accurate and believable way to say this, rather than "prayer moves mountains," is that God moves mountains, and prayer moves God. When Jesus says it will be done for them, he is saying that it isn't you or your prayer that moves the mountain but God who does the heavy lifting. Prayer lets God loose on your troubles and gives your heart rest from the fear, doubt, and worries of life.

PRAYER NOT ONLY LETS GOD LOOSE ON YOUR TROUBLES BUT ALSO LETS YOUR TROUBLES LOOSE FROM YOUR LIFE. When life is all about you, your ability, your struggle, and your strength, it can get very difficult and exhausting. Trying to manage your life yourself is like trying to balance twenty-five spinning plates on sticks—dizzying if not impossible. When you think you are all alone in this life and you have to do it all by your strength, that's when your emotions take a downhill turn. But that's not the way of the Brave. The Brave turn all their anxiety over to God, through prayer,

because they know that he not only cares for them but also can handle the impossible (see 1 Pet. 5:7).

The process of moving from fear to bravery through prayer involves what you know about God's goodness and ability, your sinfulness and inability, and prayer's purposes and necessity. **THE PURPOSE OF PRAYER IS TO GET AHOLD OF GOD, NOT HIS ANSWER.** The necessity of prayer is not only for your life but also for the lives of those around you. Prayer brings you to admit your inability and to call on his ability, and in doing that it changes you and your problems. Prayer that stays strong and determined in the face of fear and pain is prayer that reminds you of what God has given you. This part of prayer says thank you—and it says thank you for everything, not just the good but the bad as well. The words "thank you" confirm that God is good and that so is what he has let into your life. It brings your mind into alignment with truth instead of doubt and darkness. "Thank" and "you" are two powerful words in the life of prayer.

THE BRAVE THANK GOD FOR EVERYTHING (see 1 Thess. 5:18). They are able to do that because of what they know about God. But what they know about God is further reinforced through the prayer of praise. Telling God how amazing he is only reminds your heart of the same. It's like shining an enormous light on the darkness of your life—it changes everything in its light. As things around you become more clear, so does your sinfulness. The more you see God's holiness, the more you see your messiness. **THE BRAVE DON'T LET THEIR MESS BECOME THEIR DOWNFALL, THOUGH, BUT THROUGH PRAYER AND CONFESSION THEY LET THEIR MESS GO.** They know that if they confess their sins, he is faithful and just to forgive them their sins, and not only that, but to cleanse them of all unrighteousness (see 1 John 1:9). So the Brave confess and in confessing not only get forgiveness but also get a more honest perspective on their lives. Living as if your life isn't a mess, or as if your mess either isn't any fault of your own or isn't far better than what you deserve for how rotten you've been, is living a total lie. That lie is what feeds your doubt, your fear, and your worry. But an honest assessment of your failure and God's glory restores peace and hope, because it takes you off the throne of life and puts him back on.

Prayer thanks, praises, and confesses, and then prayer pleads. But the truth is that truly effective prayer doesn't plead just for itself. If the believer is consumed with the goodness of God, eventually their most urgent prayer won't be for self but will be for others. That's where real

WHOM HAVE I IN HEAVEN BUT YOU?

AND THERE IS NOTHING ON EARTH THAT I DESIRE BESIDES YOU.

MY FLESH AND MY HEART MAY FAIL,

BUT GOD IS THE STRENGTH OF MY HEART AND MY PORTION FOREVER.

FOR BEHOLD, THOSE WHO
   ARE FAR FROM YOU
   SHALL PERISH;

YOU PUT AN END TO
   EVERYONE WHO IS
   UNFAITHFUL TO YOU.

BUT FOR ME IT IS GOOD TO
   BE NEAR GOD;

I HAVE MADE THE LORD
   GOD MY REFUGE,

THAT I MAY TELL OF
   ALL YOUR WORKS.

PSALM 73:25-28 ESV

change takes place—where you go from scared to brave, from doubt to belief. A prayer that is focused entirely on you is a selfish prayer, and there is no trace of selfishness in the life of Christ. If Christ is living in you, then your prayer will naturally become less about you and more about others. This prayer is the prayer of intercession, and nowhere is it seen more beautifully rewarded than in the life of Job. In a weird twist of irony, Job spent most of the time he was suffering pleading with God to die, to be taken away from his pain, to never have been born, but it wasn't until he stopped that line of pleading and instead prayed for the lives of his friends that he was set free. Take a look at Job 42:10: "After Job prayed for his friends, the Lord restored Job's prosperity and gave him twice as much as he had before." The prayer of intercession draws us out of our little drama and into the story of God's work here on earth. It takes us away from what troubles us and puts us into a far more active and glorifying role of serving God and others.

The Brave change the subject from self to God and others. When that happens, strength is restored and purpose is found. Wallowing in your own fear and pain produces nothing but more of its kind. But refusing to accuse God and instead deciding to fight for others releases you from the stranglehold on your problems.

The Brave are less occupied with what ails them and more occupied with what can be done for others. In this subtle gift of selflessness, freedom is found, and that freedom generates bravery in your life. In his first letter to the Corinthians, Paul pens these words: "Let no one seek his own good, but the good of his neighbor" (1 Cor. 10:24 ESV).

Change the subject. *TO FIND THE BRAVE IN YOUR LIFE, CHANGE THE SUBJECT FROM YOU TO THE FATHER, FROM YOU TO OTHERS.* When you get your eyes off of your problem, it becomes much, much smaller.

THE BRAVE STUDY

The Brave are not winging it. They aren't making life up on the fly, but they have a source for knowledge and hope, and that is the Bible. The Brave study God's Word in order to know the God they love and to understand his ways and his thoughts so those will inform their choices. A little bit of Bible study with a little bit of prayer mixed in will mean death to your spiritual life. A lot of Bible study with a little bit of prayer makes for a sickly life. A lot of prayer with a little bit of Bible study gives you a healthier but inconsistent life. But *A LOT OF BIBLE STUDY WITH A*

LOT OF PRAYER MAKES FOR A BRAVE LIFE, filled with tremendous health and power. Prayer and Bible study go hand in hand in the life of the Brave.

When God tells you in Ephesians 6 to put on the armor of God, he includes the sword of the Spirit, meaning the Word of God (see v. 17). This weapon is used to cut through the lies of this world and to get us to the truth. Hebrews 4:12–13 talks about God's Word like this:

> God's word is living and active. It is sharper than any two-edged sword and cuts as deep as the place where soul and spirit meet, the place where joints and marrow meet. God's word judges a person's thoughts and intentions. No creature can hide from God. Everything is uncovered and exposed for him to see. We must answer to him.

God's Word is the weapon of choice in the fight for brave in your life. You have to search for truth, find it, and consume it whole in order for it to sink into your soul and to feed the brave in your life.

Every fear that threatens to hurt you, every doubt that tears you away from belief, all of it can find answers in God's Word. If you avoid looking into it out of the fear of not finding what you need, you're feeding the lie that life is too much for you and even God to handle. This way of thinking keeps you in darkness, but opening up the pages of your Bible and letting the Holy Spirit teach you about the Father turns on the lights and reveals places you've been tripping over again and again.

The Bible has all you need to heal all your sinful choices and even consequences. When you have an unwanted feeling in your life, a trial, or a problem, it is guaranteed that God's Word, and not a fortune cookie or palm reader, can soothe it. The Brave don't search God's thoughts *and* man's, but God's alone. Even books like this one cannot be your guide but should serve to point you to the only real source of truth, the living and active Word of God.

IF YOU THINK GOD'S WORD HAS FAILED YOU IN THE PAST, MAYBE IT'S TIME TO CONSIDER THAT IT WASN'T GOD'S WORD THAT FAILED BUT THE MIXING OF HIS WORD WITH THE WORD, OR THE THOUGHTS, OF PEOPLE. First Corinthians 1:20–21 says, "Where is the wise person? Where is the scholar? Where is the persuasive speaker of our time? Hasn't God turned the wisdom of the world into nonsense? The world with its wisdom was unable to recognize God in terms of his own wisdom." The Brave find hope in God's Word alone, and when they are given advice or something to cling to from anyone or anything other than God's Word, they run it all by the Word to see if it is consistent.

For many, bravery is fleeting or hard to come by, because they follow the ideas of people who don't base their wisdom on God's wisdom. They attempt to rise above their difficulties instead of finding God in them. They determine that the battle of life is fought on earth and not in heaven. And they trust their present and their future to the intellect and experiences of other people rather than the truth of God.

If you want brave to become a part of your life, you have to find out what God has said in his Word. Search it, scour it, read it from cover to cover. Ponder it, run through it, rest on it, sleep with it, memorize it, drill it, search it, and know that the more of it you get into you, the more brave you will have.

THE BRAVE PRACTICE SELF-CONTROL

SELF-CONTROL THAT DOESN'T COME FROM THE SPIRIT OF GOD LIVING IN YOU IS TEMPORARY, fleeting, and offers a form of courage founded in human strength and conviction. But the self-control the Bible speaks of is a gift from God, and therefore it isn't found in the strength of people. Second Timothy 1:7 confirms that "God gave us a spirit not of fear but of power and love and self-control" (ESV). And in Galatians 5:23, self-control is listed as a fruit that grows from the Spirit. While self-control involves your will, more importantly, it involves the will of the Spirit living in you. That means that up until now, you may have had very little self-control. You might have had a hard time not freaking out when danger comes your way or not breaking down when heartache threatens to tear you up. When bad things happen to you or around you, you might not have a good track record of calm self-control, but that doesn't mean that with a little knowledge added to your life you can't get all the self-control you need.

How easy it is to think that self-control is all about "self." It's in the word, after all! That's really not all it's about, though. Certainly self-control requires something of you, but it might not require as much as you think. The key to self-control is faith. You have to have faith that God has the ability to give you the self-control he promises. All the virtues that make up the fruit of the Spirit grow not out of your own goodness but out of the goodness of the Holy Spirit himself, who takes up residence in you at the time when you accept Christ as your Savior. In order to access the fruit, including self-control, you simply have to call on God himself for the outpouring of his Spirit on your life.

First of all, self-control has to be your desire. You have to agree with God that what you are lacking

in the area of courage, confidence, hope, and calm self-control is what you need, and then you have to simply ask him for it. Remember, Jesus said, "If you live in me and what I say lives in you, then ask for anything you want, and it will be yours" (John 15:7). Sound preposterous? Really, what is he, a sugar daddy who gives you whatever you ask for? Perhaps, but with one requirement on that: what you ask has to be consistent with holiness. It has to be for your best, not for your pleasure alone. James 4:3 says the lack of real and sustainable change in your life is because of this: "When you pray for things, you don't get them because you want them for the wrong reason—for your own pleasure." There are a lot of things that don't make their way into your life because of the reasons you want them. But when you pray for obedience or wisdom, the things within God's perfect will for your life, you can be sure that Jesus's words ring true: you will get whatever you ask for, because it's exactly what he's written that he will give you. See the correlation? **PRAY FOR WHAT GOD HAS ALREADY PROMISED YOU—"LOVE, JOY, PEACE, PATIENCE, KINDNESS, GOODNESS, FAITHFULNESS, GENTLENESS, AND SELF-CONTROL" (GAL. 5:22-23)—AND IT WILL BE YOURS.**

THE BRAVE CONQUER THEIR FEAR

Self-control is God's gift to you, just waiting to be taken, opened up, and put on. It is already yours; you just need to take it. The brave in your life will be fed, sustained, and kept forever through the self-control that God gives to you through his Holy Spirit. In the words of Paul, "practice self-control, and keep your minds clear so that you can pray" (1 Pet. 4:7). Brave will be a part of your life once you accept the self-control given you from the hands of God.

THE BRAVE SING

Martin Luther said that *"MUSIC DRIVES AWAY THE DEVIL."* Singing has a powerful effect not only on the singer but also on the hearers, and singing songs that worship the Father makes all that is unholy scurry away. In the face of terror, danger, fear, or emotional turmoil, nothing soothes as well as singing of God's goodness. After being attacked by angry men, while officials looked on and then joined in, Paul and Silas were thrown into a damp, dirty, rat-infested jail cell and chained up in a bloody heap, not knowing what fate would await them at daybreak. Their condition was horrible, their pain unbearable, and their response incredible. Instead of crying in agony or plotting their resistance, they did

the unthinkable: they sang songs. Just take a look at the scene in Acts 16:25–26:

> Around midnight Paul and Silas were praying and sing-
> ing hymns of praise to God. The other prisoners were
> listening to them. Suddenly, a violent earthquake shook
> the foundations of the jail. All the doors immediately
> flew open, and all the prisoners' chains came loose.

Did you see that? The danger and pain of being held, chained up, in a first-century prison were overcome not by attorneys or secret late-night breakouts by brave resistance fighters but by singing—by worshiping the God who allowed it all to happen.

This is evidence that in the fight for their lives, the Brave sing. Music has a powerful effect on the human soul, it is true, but when the songs declare the power and the glory of God, when they praise and worship our Creator, the effect is spiritually life changing. There are times in life when the enemy attacks, when the flesh is weak, and when nature takes control, and nothing else can overcome these as well as worship—the act of praising God with song. In fact, in Scripture there are even times, such as when Paul and Silas were in prison, when God literally moves into action upon hearing the songs of his people. In 2 Chronicles 20:21–22, the battle is raging between God's people and his enemies. In just another great example of how God uses music to fight battles, we read this:

> After he [Jehoshaphat] had advised the people, he appointed people to sing to the Lord and praise him for the beauty of his holiness. As they went in front of the troops, they sang, "Thank the Lord because his mercy endures forever!" As they started to sing praises, the Lord set ambushes against the Ammonites, Moabites, and the people of Mount Seir who had come into Judah. They were defeated.

WORSHIP MUSIC SQUEEZES OUT OF US THE TOXIC THINGS THAT AREN'T FROM GOD, LIKE FEAR, WORRY, AND DOUBT. They are all removed on the wings of worship. The Brave know that in times of severe testing and trial, worship is the only cure, because it communicates God's presence to your soul and to the situation, and it warns the voices that can plague the fearful that God will not be abandoned or forgotten but is to be relied on and worshiped. And nothing makes the enemy more angry than a child of God who worships.

What makes the Brave different from the rest of the world is the God they worship. His power, his presence, and his Spirit inside them give them all the power and self-control they need to withstand any testing or trial.

The Brave are really weak and scared people who refuse to let that be the end of the story but insist it is only the beginning. The Brave distinguish themselves best by their faith. They have a faith that is secure and will not be moved by the rising tide or the crumbling of mountains. The Brave don't see through purely physical eyes but through spiritual eyes, recognizing that in everything in their lives the hand of God is active and gracious, compassionate and sure. They bank their lives on his goodness and grace, knowing that nothing can separate them from his love—not death or life, not angels or rulers, nothing in the present or in the future, not forces or powers in the world above or in the world below—nothing in all creation can separate them from God's love (see Rom. 8:38–39). Of this they are sure, and so they can be a part of the brave few who stand when trials come, who smile when pain hits, who pray when doubt creeps in, and who worship when life threatens to destroy.

The Brave are the few who have the courage to believe and not doubt, even when their flesh screams otherwise, and because of that the Brave are blessed. They are given all they need for any situation they are in, living in peace and contentment with nothing but the Father above and his Spirit within.

OSWALD CHAMBERS WROTE, "ALL OUR FEARS ARE WICKED, AND WE FEAR BECAUSE WE WILL NOT NOURISH OURSELVES IN OUR FAITH.** How can anyone who is identified with Jesus Christ suffer from doubt or fear! It ought to be an absolute psalm of perfectly irrepressible, triumphant belief."[9] You weren't meant to fear the things of this world. To fear what God controls is to doubt his goodness, but to be brave is to trust his omnipotence. Only your fear of God will overpower your fears that cripple and paralyze you.

Your life will attract whatever it fears. Fear failure, and you'll find failure. Fear danger, and that's what you will find all around you. Fear God, and you will find yourself in love with the best of beings and brave beyond belief. You attract, see, and are surrounded by whatever you fear, and that fear will color all of your other actions. But fear doesn't have to be a bad thing—not for the Brave.

You can become one of the Brave. All it takes is a simple faith, even just the size of a mustard seed, in the God of the Bible. Your pain may linger, your trials may crush, but fear not, for God is with you. He's been there all along; maybe you just haven't noticed him or known enough about him. He is present to save you and to rescue you from this world. Can you trust him? Will you trust him today with your pain, your fear, and your suffering? If you keep doing what you're doing, you'll keep getting what you're getting. If that isn't enough, then make a change today and start doing something for the brave in you. Start believing in the saving power of Christ not only for your salvation for heaven but also for your salvation through the fire.

When you put fear in the right place by rejecting the terrors of this world, you will soon find that nothing can separate you from the love of God: "neither death nor life, nor angels nor rulers, nor things present nor things to come, nor powers, nor height nor depth, nor anything else in all creation, will be able to separate us from the love of God in Christ Jesus our Lord" (Rom. 8:38–39 ESV). In this love the Brave find all the strength they need. Will you join the ranks of the Brave?

When you put fear into perspective, fearing the right thing and trusting all the rest to be within God's control and will, then nothing can harm you. To become brave, turn your mind over to God, know him, become familiar with his ways, study his Word, and find out about his nature. Make all of this the most important stuff in your life, and you will be part of the Brave!

DON'T YOU KNOW THAT ALL OF US WHO WERE BAPTIZED INTO CHRIST JESUS WERE BAPTIZED INTO HIS DEATH? WHEN WE WERE BAPTIZED INTO HIS DEATH, WE WERE PLACED INTO THE TOMB WITH HIM. AS CHRIST WAS BROUGHT BACK FROM DEATH TO LIFE BY THE GLORIOUS POWER OF THE FATHER, SO WE, TOO, SHOULD LIVE A NEW KIND OF LIFE.

IF WE'VE BECOME UNITED
WITH HIM IN A DEATH LIKE HIS,
CERTAINLY WE WILL ALSO BE
UNITED WITH HIM WHEN WE COME
BACK TO LIFE AS HE DID. WE
KNOW THAT THE PERSON WE
USED TO BE WAS CRUCIFIED WITH
HIM TO PUT AN END TO SIN IN
OUR BODIES. BECAUSE OF THIS
WE ARE NO LONGER SLAVES TO
SIN. THE PERSON WHO HAS DIED
HAS BEEN FREED FROM SIN.

ROMANS 6:3-7

NOTES

1. *Braveheart*, directed by Mel Gibson (1995; Hollywood, CA: Paramount Home Video, 2004), DVD.

2. Hannah Hurnard, *Hinds' Feet on High Places* (Wheaton: Tyndale, 1979), 168.

3. Darrel W. Amundsen, "The Anguish and Agonies of Charles Spurgeon," *Christian History* 29, no. 1 (January 1991), 25.

4. C. H. Spurgeon, "The Minister in These Times," sermon text available online at the Spurgeon Archive, http://www.spurgeon.org/misc/aarm12.htm.

5. Shawn Achor, "Make Stress Work for You," *Harvard Business Review*, February 15, 2011, http://blogs.hbr.org/cs/2011/02/make_stress_work_for_you.html.

6. C. H. Spurgeon, "Contentment," sermon text available online at the Spurgeon Archive, http://www.spurgeon.org/sermons/0320.htm.

7. Divorce is a sin unless there has been adultery or abandonment. All other excuses for divorce are considered unacceptable by God (Matt. 19:8–9; 1 Cor. 7:10–15).

8. E. M. Bounds, *The Necessity of Prayer*, available online at the Christian Classics Ethereal Library, http://www.ccel.org/browse/bookInfo?id=bounds/necessity.

9. Oswald Chambers, *My Utmost for His Highest: Selections for the Year* (Grand Rapids: Discovery House Publishers, 1993), November 13.

Hayley DiMarco is founder of Hungry Planet, where she writes and creates cutting-edge books that connect with the multitasking mind-set. She has written and cowritten numerous bestselling books for both teens and adults, including *God Girl*, *Devotions for the God Girl*, *Mean Girls*, *B4UD8*, and *Die Young*.

Michael DiMarco is the publisher and creative director of Hungry Planet. He has written and cowritten numerous bestselling books for both teens and adults, including *God Guy*, *Devotions for the God Guy*, *B4UD8*, *Unstuff*, *Almost Sex*, and *Die Young*.

Michael and Hayley live with their daughter in Nashville, Tennessee.

The *Ultimate Bible* just for the *God Girl!*

It's a blank canvas—design your own cover! Download patterns and stencils at GodGirl.com.

With special features like Ask Yourself, Prayers, God Girl Stories, and Know This Devotions, all written by bestselling author Hayley DiMarco, the *God Girl Bible* is a must-have for girls thirteen and up! If you're ready to grow closer to God, grow in your faith, and join an on-line group of girls from around the globe growing together, the *God Girl Bible* is for you!

Available Wherever Books Are Sold

Revell
a division of Baker Publishing Group
www.RevellBooks.com

Hungry Planet
www.hungryplanet.net

GodGirl.com

Become the Man God Created You to Be

When you become a God Guy, your life will never be the same.

Available Wherever Books Are Sold

The Ultimate Bible just for the God Guy!

Combining the clear everyday language of GOD'S WORD Translation
with inspirational writing from bestselling author Michael DiMarco, the
God Guy Bible is jam-packed with timeless features.

Available Wherever Books Are Sold

It's time to put your past in its place.

It's easy to get hung up on things that happened yesterday,
or last week, or last year. But with God's help, you don't have
to let guilt, bitterness, resentment, or fear rule your life.

Available Wherever Books Are Sold

Breaking free from the things that consume you

Obsessed

breaking free from the
things that consume you

Hayley DiMarco
Bestselling author of *God Girl*

Are you obsessed? We can all feel that way at times—when
every bit of our thoughts, time, and energy are poured into something
all-consuming. But those things can get between you and God.
Hayley will show you how putting things in their proper place
helps you become rightly obsessed with God.

Available Wherever Books Are Sold

Dating or waiting?
First date or 500th?

B4UD8

7 THINGS YOU NEED TO KNOW **BEFORE** YOUR NEXT DATE

HAYLEY & MICHAEL **DiMARCO**

Hungry Planet tells you everything you need to know.

Available Wherever Books Are Sold